Follow the Money

Follow the Money

A Guide to Exploring the Last Taboo Topic with Your Clients

Judith Stern Peck and Betsy Witten

BLOOMSBURY ACADEMIC
NEW YORK • LONDON • OXFORD • NEW DELHI • SYDNEY

BLOOMSBURY ACADEMIC
Bloomsbury Publishing Inc, 1359 Broadway, New York, NY 10018, USA
Bloomsbury Publishing Plc, 50 Bedford Square, London, WC1B 3DP, UK
Bloomsbury Publishing Ireland, 29 Earlsfort Terrace, Dublin 2, D02 AY28, Ireland

BLOOMSBURY, BLOOMSBURY ACADEMIC and the Diana logo are trademarks of Bloomsbury Publishing Plc

First published in the United States of America 2025

Cover design: Dustin Watson

A catalog record for this book is available from the Library of Congress.

ISBN: HB: 978-1-5381-8350-2
PB: 978-1-5381-8351-9
ePDF: 979-8-7651-5451-9
eBook: 978-1-5381-8352-6

Typeset by Deanta Global Publishing Services, Chennai, India

For product safety related questions contact productsafety@bloomsbury.com.

To find out more about our authors and books visit www.bloomsbury.com and sign up for our newsletters.

Contents

About the Authors

Judith Stern Peck, LCSW, has extensive experience as both a family therapist and a consultant to family businesses, family foundations, and family offices. She is director of a project team at the Ackerman Institute for the Family that researches, educates, and consults on Money and Family Life, and the author of *Money and Meaning: New Ways to Have Conversations with Clients about Money* (Wiley, 2007). She is also principal of JSP Associates, a firm that provides educational and consultation services to family businesses, family foundations, and family offices. Her educational background includes a BA from Finch College and an MSW from Yeshiva University. She attended the Ackerman Institute for the Family for her post-graduate training.

Betsy Witten, JD, is a New York–based coach who helps clients develop self-awareness and agency around money. She supports their navigation of legal and investment relationships through life-cycle transitions including trust creation, estate planning, and pre- and post-nuptial agreements. Her professional history includes being an attorney, a social justice advocate, a founder of a high school for court-involved students, and a Program Director at a national foundation. She has co-facilitated the Money and Meaning Workshop at the Ackerman Institute for the Family. Betsy received both her BA and JD from Columbia University.

Preface

People talk about money all the time. We watch *Million Dollar Listings* and *Succession* and we talk to our friends about the price of groceries, but no one really *talks* about money. There is a nearly universal taboo on talking about what money actually *signifies* to individuals, for example safety, a connection to the past, love, or self-worth. The taboo is equally strong when it comes to talking about the *practicalities* of money, for example our earnings, our debt, or our wealth. In every culture and every era, there are topics that are taboo. Right now in the United States, people are willing to talk about sex, about religion, even about politics. But they will not talk about money.

Certain other aspects of the self—Gender, Sexuality, Race, Illness, Mental Illness—were historically taboo subjects in "majority culture," leading families and individuals to be secretive and to feel isolated. All these aspects have become more broadly and commonly discussed and more fully integrated into the individual sense of self. Each of these areas of exploration has been expanded within the mental health world both practically and theoretically.

Healthy family functioning and healthy relational functioning depend on how open people are to having conversations in these areas. The previous secretiveness and shame were corrosive to relational health as they inhibited people from developing relational communication skills.

As our culture shifted from treating each of these areas as taboo to more openness and integration, each aspect of identity required common language to discuss it, and mechanisms for raising consciousness so that the full self could be seen and discussed. As each taboo subject area was incorporated into therapeutic practice, therapists had to examine themselves, and had to develop comfort and skill discussing something they themselves might have found taboo. Therapists had to get comfortable with the new language and new ideas in order to integrate them and apply them to their work.

It is interesting to consider how and why money and class became and remain taboo topics in the United States, and we hope this book might prompt more discussion of the question. Our understanding and experience is that this social prohibition is not universal and that there are countries in which discussions of money and class are more open. It seems especially strange that our society has a taboo about discussing money when we live in a capitalist economy, where money is the coin of the realm. Money is the value we attach to things, activities, and services. It should come as no surprise that money is also how we learn to measure other things—love, power, our value as people, each other's value as people. We wonder if there is a relationship between money being everywhere in our society—while simultaneously being nowhere in our conversations.

We are curious to understand the role of increasing economic inequality on the societal prohibition against talking about money. Some research has indicated that people feel happier when they socialize or live around people with the same economic circumstances. We hope further research is done to explore whether there are other cultures and countries in which there is less secretiveness and taboo around money, and if so, to understand why. Within American capitalism however we are seeing a clear story. In a time of (1) income inequality and (2) racial and gender financial inequality, again it seems obvious to wonder if there is a concomitant internalizing of the value placed on the labor and circumstance of women and people of color according to identity. It may be that Americans internalize shame whether they have less than they need or more than they need, whether they have a little, or a lot.

To move our culture and our families/clients into healthier relational dynamics we believe they need to become conscious of the role of money and class in their lives, and to become aware of the parts of their identities that they have avoided discussing and exploring.

How do we start to discuss this important thread in our clients' lives?

Therapy is a joint venture between therapist and client in discerning what is real. Our theory of how to arrive at that stems from our own individual paths. Judith has been a family and couples' therapist for decades. Betsy became a coach more recently, bringing years of meditation, advising her community, and working on issues of money and relationships within her own family. We have the same goals regarding the discernment of reality. We both want clients to recognize their fullest truest selves and to develop their own agency, and for therapists to be sufficiently resourced to help clients achieve this recognition and agency.

We titled this book *Follow the Money* because we believe that by following—fully exploring—the thread of money in our clients' lives they can arrive at a clearer picture of what is real, and a deeper understanding of themselves. We follow the money to neutralize the charge of talking about money. We discuss money to find out what is real and what is the premise or the story in someone's mind. We follow the money as a means of exploring self, class identity, family legacies, and internal monologues. We follow the money to find clients' relational dynamics. It is an enormously powerful rich source for self-awareness.

Follow the Money does not propose a new form of therapy. We mean simply to support an under-developed topic within established frameworks. We are working on integrating money and class into Family Systems work, into the sense of self for both therapist and client, and into the work of distinguishing between the powerful stories in our heads and what is real.

Introduction

Gene was an early participant in our workshop. He had left early because of a conflict but asked if he could retake the workshop. We agreed. A few months later, when he was able to return, he shared his motivation for taking the workshop. He told us that while he and his husband were fairly comfortable discussing 'who would pay for what', they did not have a budget or 'discuss any long term planning'. In the work context he tended to delay his billing, not engage with fee increases, and not keep his receivables up to date. He suspected a psychological blockage and wanted to get to the heart of it. He also noticed that he avoided talk about money in his clinical work. He was avoiding money in every aspect of his professional life. He needed to get to the heart of this problem. When he left the initial workshop, he realized from the beginning exercises just how helpful the experience would be for him. He returned with great enthusiasm.

How can a clinician shift away from money being a subject that both the practitioner and client avoid, and create an environment in which practitioner and client can openly discuss and fully explore it? How can a clinician use money as an access point, a window into deeper understanding of the psychological underpinnings, a couple's relational dynamic?

What could we do to jump-start this process, to raise awareness and consciousness of money and identity, and to chisel away at the defenses?

Judy and Betsy met quite serendipitously hiking in the Berkshires. When they had a chance to get to know each other, it became very clear that they shared a common agenda. They both wanted to help people have realistic and productive conversations about money. Judy had been the Director of the Money and Family Life research project at the Ackerman Institute for the Family since 2000. Betsy had an early career as a lawyer. She then worked in the social justice field, advocating on behalf of and founding a high school for students coming out of the juvenile justice system. When she met Judy, she was overseeing her own family's business. Ultimately, after exploring various options for working together, they decided to develop an intensive workshop to enable participants to break through their barriers around money. It was another step in the research project to get therapists to talk about money and help their clients do the same. It presented another access point to break the taboo of money talk. Could an intensive workshop about money shift the awareness and understanding about the meaning of money in one's life? What format would work?

The ideas promoted in this book were generated by the research of the Money and Family Life project at the Ackerman Institute led by Judith Stern Peck. In the initial stages, the research team found that introducing values was a safe language to break through the taboo of money talk in families. This language of values served to neutralize families' reactivity when talking about money. The following timeline presents that history and the various phases of the Money and Family Life research outcomes. These ideas generated by the qualitative research became the foundation for the development of an intensive experiential workshop format with the goal of helping participants develop agency around money. Here is the timeline of the research project to give you a sense of the evolution of ideas and stepping stones that led to the workshop design.

Money and Family Life Project: History, Timeline and Outcomes

2000–2007

In 2000–2007, an interdisciplinary group of family therapists, family business consultants, and an investment advisor with family systems training worked collaboratively to explore commonalities learned from their work. The group (Dr. Peter Steinglass; Marcia Sheinberg; Scott Budge, PhD; Sally Wigutow; Susan Burden; Shira Ronen; Greg Roger; Elizabeth Bailey) were people both from within and outside Ackerman. They produced two books, *Money and Meaning: New Ways to Have Conversations About Money with Your Clients* by Judith Stern Peck and *The New Financial Advisor: Strategies for Successful Family Wealth Management* by G. Scott Budge, PhD. Both books address the taboo of money talk and attempt in different ways to give the professionals addressed in each book ways to facilitate and shift conversations around money and family. It was just the beginning of breaking down the taboo of money talk.

2008–2014

For the next seven years, Judy worked with a colleague, Markie Sallik, in the Ackerman clinic seeing couples where money presented as a problem.

Their work led to talking about money in the clinical space as an access point for identifying the relational dynamic and underlying issues. Together, they developed an all-day workshop on couples therapy and money, highlighting the process of tracking the money, collecting the financial information, discovering the dynamic, and shifting from the emotional issues to the practical to begin to surface the underlying premises and meaning. This ability to move from the practical to the emotional comes with comfort and confidence in both arenas.

2017–Present

When Judy and Betsy met in 2016, they immediately bonded around their shared goal: getting people to break through the taboo of money talk and helping participants develop agency around money. By agency, they mean the ability to make their own decisions, shape their own lives, which depends on the ability to talk about money rather than avoiding it,, and to take responsibility for the financial dimension of their lives. To that end, they designed an intensive experiential workshop format around money talk. Their belief was that in order to get to agency they had to start with awareness. They developed exercises that both surfaced repeated internal language and patterns of behavior that were connected to money. These interactive group discussions lead to the final and ultimate exercise, the money-focused genogram, a tool to explore and deepen clients' awareness of their relationship to money. It is a tool to unfold a historic look through a money-focused multigenerational mapping that surfaces the transmission of premises and patterns around money, work and class. We anticipated that doing this exercise with participants would certainly bring them to the state of awareness we were seeking. It would allow for a perspective that might widen the lens and give them more openness to money exploration. The challenge in doing this was to create a safe space that allowed for personal vulnerabilities to surface during the genogram mapping.

The original workshop spanned a day and a half and included a didactic component about budgets and investing. Our participants were recruited from our own personal networks. By 2018, we had facilitated eight of these workshops and had sixty participants. Our ambition was to bring awareness to participants of the thread of money in their thinking, and to open up the possibility of a change in attitude or behavoir around money. We did a survey to research the impact on participants. The results were quite remarkable. 65 percent of participants responded and 47 percent said there had been change in their attitude or behavior around money, how they thought about money or dealt with money. With this information in hand, Judy advocated for offering the workshop through the Ackerman website.

This changed the population to mostly mental health professionals. It also meant condensing the workshop to one six-hour day, including content about fees and the business of one's practice. We made those changes easily by dropping the financial literacy component.

To date, we have facilitated 18–20 workshops for mental health practitioners, which brings the number of participants to 200 people. The Ackerman format requires that participants fill out an evaluation form at the end of the workshop. Those forms have shown resoundingly high levels of satisfaction which we understand as showing us that the experience of the workshop as being overwhelmingly successful in its objective of breaking the taboo of money talk. With this in mind, we are writing this book to expand the universe of people who can talk about money with their clients in greater depth and increased understanding of the myriads of its meanings. We are writing this book to support your offering the experience within your community and/or beginning to break the silence of money within your own practice.

New Equipment for Therapeutic Toolbox

Money remains a taboo subject for many mental health professionals. This workshop experience can be the catalyst for changing that! It requires a two-pronged approach. First and foremost, everything begins with an exploration of one's own money identity as well as one's relational dynamic around money. Once these issues become clearer and neutralized, it is time to begin to use it in your clinical work. It is a new access point rather than a new model.

When we use the word "neutralized" around money talk, we mean that the conflictual emotional attachments are dissipated, and money can be talked about without the emotional charge. Individuals and families can make money-related decisions based on values that a family/couple shares with clear communication to all concerned. And for the clinician, money—like sex—can be used as a theme to access deeper meaning and relational dynamics.

Throughout the years of exploring the interface of money and family, we have come to respect the complexity of money in our society and the multiple meanings people attach to it. Shedding these threads can take a long time. Our workshop has proven to be an effective beginning for this process. The use of the money-focused genogram as a tool/centerpiece stimulates the change process and has proven to be effective and efficient. The challenge of doing this in a small group setting and having participants feel safe enough to expose vulnerabilities was accomplished by the creation of a safe space. We are pleased to have the opportunity to describe to you the sequence of experiential exercises as well as our thinking that informed it.

Here are the premises for the process that informed our thinking.

Our Operating Principles for the Process

1. Know Your Money/Class Identity
   Facilitating conversations about money is an art, not a science. What do we mean? Because everyone carries a confluence of meanings of money, it is important first and foremost to learn about your own money/class identity and the emotional attachments you hold to each. These might shift under different circumstances. Understanding when and where they surface and interfere with your neutrality is key to enabling you to have thoughtful, constructive and informative money-related conversations.
2. Respect money and its complexity
   Explore your embedded biases around money/class and the premises you hold about wealth, privilege or poverty. Approach the conversation with curiosity and respect. Be aware of your own reactivity to what you are hearing. Understand how class might play a role. Hold compassion for the varied stories that will unfold.
3. Safety of environment
   Create a nonjudgmental space with compassion, curiosity and collaboration as its base. At the same time, use your internal professional assessment to deal with the interruptions or detours that occur. Managing the "climate" of the group is key to the ultimate outcome.
4. Neutrality of language
   Be comfortable with financial language, that is income, budget, cashflow, net worth, deficit, interest rate, trusts, taxes, etc. Start with the basics needed for maintaining a family's household, that is rent, utilities, food, etc. Explore sources of the income. This is the factual part of the conversation.

How to Use this Book

This book is divided into three parts. Part 1 has two chapters. The first chapter presents the theoretical framework for both the content and process of the workshop design. The second chapter describes the fundamentals for creating a safe space both practically and emotionally, reviewing the basic criteria as well as the pacing and sequencing of the exercises. Whether you are looking to replicate the workshop or just choosing the book as a self-study exercise, part one provides the foundation.

Part 2 describes the interactive exercises with a step-by-step description. It also includes case examples compiled from real participants. Chapter 3, 4, 5, and 6 describe the details of the exercises. Chapter 7 offers a map for taking the workshop yourself. It gives you a step-by-step process for your self-exploration. Part Three goes over the integration and application of these ideas into your practice and provides case reviews using family life cycle transitions as a frame. These show how using the access to money facilitated a treatment process to underlying meaning and change.

This workshop is new and innovative. It has proven to be a successful catalyst for breaking through the defenses around money. Money is such an integral part of our lives and yet most people avoid talking about it. This workshop has helped so many to break through that taboo of money talk. From our experience and research, this ability will impact the quality of family functioning and provide a healthier attitude for the money talk!

Gene presented his family membership. His parents were married for thirty-six years. His younger brother was pursuing a career in the theater. He was also receiving an allowance! Since Gene graduated and started to pursue his clinical practice his father had committed to a monthly allowance. About three months ago, his father sent him an email that it was time for Gene to become financially independent. He was going to cut back the allowance incrementally over the next nine months now that Gene was on his way professionally. There was little to no discussion about how this might work. Although Gene did not disagree with the premise of financial independence, he was puzzled by how his father presented it and when he attempted to have conversations about it, his Dad just kept restating the goals. Gene was also quite anxious about how he might manage financially going forward and realized that he needed to get more comfortable with money management.

In facilitating Gene's money-focused genogram, we discovered that his parents had never talked about money or even given Gene and his brother an allowance of any sort. Gene had never really worked before setting up his practice. There was never any "money talk" in the family. His grandparents had immigrated to the States, worked hard and both his parents had become doctors. His father had worked to supplement family income during his teenage years. Throughout their professional lives, Gene's parents had both worked and provided the family a comfortable lifestyle. There had been little to no discussion about money in Gene's family, but money was always there! As we mapped this family history, Gene looked at the board and recognized the multigenerational dependency theme that popped out for him: his grandparent's dependency on his parents and his dependency on them as well. He wondered if his parents understood what had happened here. The mystery was beginning to unravel. Gene could now have a more open conversation with his mom and dad. They all shared the same goal. They just needed to address the way to get there.

Section One

Theory and Design for Workshop

Foundational Concepts

1

As mentioned in the introduction, we met serendipitously. We immediately understood our point of connection to be "money talk" by which we mean the ability to discuss the practicalities of money and higher level 'finances', as well as the emotional and relational issues around money. Although we came from different professional disciplines, we shared a common objective: to break the taboo of money talk within families. How could we get people to develop this consciousness? We both understood from our own experiences with "money talk" that while everyone has a relationship with money, people often lack awareness of this relationship, and that lack of awareness stands in the way of their developing true agency regarding money. We also understood that people have an inherent resistance to money talk. Our challenge was both breaking through that resistance and facilitating change.

After much deliberation, we decided to develop an intensive workshop that would trigger a process for participants to develop an in-depth self-understanding around money. Through our own professional and personal experiences, we knew that we could help people develop this awareness and agency around money while working one-on-one. We wanted to know if we could achieve the same results with more people in a shorter period. We were curious about how to take that process to scale with a group. We wanted to reach more people. We knew from experience that working in a group context had additional benefits. We thought a group format would provide the shared experience and help to break through the personal/individual barriers to money talk. The more challenging question was how to facilitate an intensive workshop in a short amount of time and get people to be uncomfortable and vulnerable enough to look at and talk about money, a very taboo subject for most people.

We created our workshop to explore the question of whether an intensive workshop experience could be the catalyst for changing a person's relationship to money, and specifically for increasing their awareness and their agency. We see awareness as one's thought process and consideration of money as an issue. When we use the term agency, we mean a person's ability to make their own decisions, shape their own lives, with confidence in one's ability to handle a range of financial tasks and situations. Our objective for the workshop was for participants to begin to change their attitudes and/or behaviors with this confidence. The following list of objectives served as our guide in working toward that change.

1. Invite conversation and exploration of money and meaning in a neutral and safe environment.
2. Follow the thread of money and money/class identity through a multigenerational mapping of relational patterns and family history.

3. Gain a greater understanding of one's money identity to offer a fuller location of self[1] around class and economic circumstance.
4. Feel more at ease in having open, neutral discussions about money, including talking about fees with clients and discussing family finances with a partner.

We decided to use a group setting in part because we wanted to reach more people, and we believed that hearing stories from others with a range of experiences, both similar and dissimilar to one's own, would positively impact change. We also understood that a group experience could begin to counter the isolation, shame, and insecurity that often inhibit one's money identity.

Initially, we tested out the format and idea with a diverse group we gathered through our own networks. After facilitating a handful of workshops, we surveyed participants on the experience and received very positive results. We were then given the opportunity to promote the workshop through the Ackerman Institute website. Because of this, most of the participants in the workshops that followed were mental health professionals. We were excited to work with this population because we both wanted to help them break the silence around money in the clinical space, and we also hoped that they might then be able to replicate the workshop in their respective communities. If the workshop could help them acknowledge the complex role money plays in their own families, it would heighten their knowledge and appreciation of the information they could gather in the clinical space around "money." In addition, it would give clinicians another pathway to the underlying clinical material. That ripple effect would broaden the impact of the workshop. With this shift of constituents, we changed the timing, not the content, and added a vignette or two to promote conversation about fees and collection policy.

In developing the format for the workshop, we continually revisited how best to ignite and facilitate this change process. We chose an experiential rather than a didactic format. Instead of lecturing, we facilitated interactive exercises.

We wanted to stimulate as much conversation as possible among the group that would highlight deep-seated beliefs about money. We wanted to talk with participants rather than talking at them. We understood that stimulating participants' thought processes through conversations would be more effective than lecture.

1 Location of self is the name of a process in which the therapist initiates a conversation with a family about similarities and differences in their key identities, such as race, ethnicity, gender, class, sexual orientation, and religion, and how they may potentially influence the therapy process.

We consistently asked for feedback from participants and incorporated changes where we felt it would be productive. We worked as co-facilitators. We created a safe environment using exercises we developed to combat the inherent resistance to money conversations. These interactive exercises, along with the ensuing conversations, surface ideas and premises around money and enable conflicts and contradictions to emerge. Throughout the daylong workshop, we pair people for conversation. We debrief as a group, and we explore individual positions. These all lead to a money-focused genogram exercise, where each person looks at his or her family history around money, work, and class. These conversations look at the money issue in varied ways and aim to begin neutralizing whatever "money taboo" each participant walked in with. Ultimately, we configure the time so that each participant thinks about, talks about, and reflects on his or her relationship to money and where those ideas come from. The pacing and configurations of these conversations chip away at the resistance and raise awareness. Early on during our time running these workshops, we discovered through feedback that this experiential process raises participants' awareness enough to begin to shift their attitudes or behaviors around money, which is the objective of the workshop.

Our intention in this chapter is to highlight the theoretical and practical ideas that underlie the design and format of the workshop. These come from the different disciplines and experiences that we both bring to the workshop—most prominently, the Ackerman Relational Approach, meditation, and our years of personal and professional experience in teaching, consulting, coaching, and counseling.

The foundational ideas and concepts for our "process" come from our different backgrounds. As a senior faculty member at the Ackerman Institute for the Family, Judy practices the Ackerman Relational Approach (ARA) in both her clinical and consulting practices, an approach developed at the Ackerman Institute that will be discussed in the next section. Betsy has a law degree and feels extremely comfortable with money talk, both practically and emotionally. She has also studied mindfulness for a long time and brings ideas stemming from mindfulness meditation into our workshop format. Importantly, we also draw on the work of Monica McGoldrick and Randy Gerson, whose ideas stem from Murray Bowen's family systems theory. We do this in our use of a money-focused genogram, which is an iteration of the genogram format developed by Monica McGoldrick and Randy Gerson in their book *Genograms: Assessment and Treatment.* A genogram, an emotional mapping of the family using a multigenerational format, is familiar to many practitioners. It provides a visual rendition of patterns and themes within a family, along with the relational dynamics.

The money-focused genogram we developed and use in the workshop is a "limited and focused version" with money, work, and class as the primary areas of exploration.

Our intention in this chapter is to explain the thinking and planning behind our approach. We reference and expand on concepts that have influenced the development of the workshop. These include the ARA theoretical and clinical concepts, facilitation ideas, and meditation concepts. All of these are relevant to the foundational design of the workshop and will be addressed here.

The Ackerman Relational Approach

The Ackerman Relational Approach is a conceptual framework for developing clinical processes that was developed by the Ackerman Institute faculty starting in 2002 and published for use in the training program in 2015. Marcia Sheinberg, then Director of Training, led the conceptualization and the creation of a manual in collaboration with Mary Kim Brewster, a senior faculty member.

As the ARA manual describes the model, it "is a systemic approach to therapy that is designed to strengthen and clarify relationships between couples and family members." This approach "includes a broad interpersonal perspective that uses a multigenerational lens as well as a cultural and social context, a horizontal, vertical, and circular view." In short, the ARA is a way of working clinically to enhance, clarify, and nurture relational bonds. It gives a specific focus of attention with multiple avenues of entry.

We avoid a "one-size-fits-all" approach and, instead, over the years, have compiled and developed, a collection of theories, ideas and practices that guide our thinking and clinical work.

To narrow our focus of the ARA for the design of the workshop, these are the specific concepts that serve as the workshop foundation. These include Bowenian systemic theory, feminist theory, narrative/social constructionist ideas, and class. A short description of each is helpful in explaining the workshop design.

1. ARA Manual Revision, Mary Kim Brewster and Marcia Sheinberg, Ackerman Institute, New York, September 2015.

Bowenian Systemic Theory

Bowenian systemic theory looks at emotional relational structures and the multigenerational transmission of patterns, themes, and roles. (Bowen,

1978). We apply this school of thought throughout the workshop—from the first moments when we ask participants to listen to their families' voices in their heads to the end of the workshop when we facilitate the money-focused genogram. The multigenerational transmission of patterns, themes, and roles is discussed in more detail in Chapter 6. The money-focused genogram offers a graphic picture that often stimulates participants to visually see the transmission.

Feminist Theory and Narrative/Social Constructionist Ideas

The workshop also incorporates basic ideas from feminist theory and narrative/social constructionist theory (Sheinberg, 1992). We often see that gendered ideas and patterns have played a role in participants' lives around money. We refer to this as socially gendered roles. For instance, when roles and responsibilities are assigned because of someone's gender rather than competence, we question that assignment. We wonder why men are mostly in charge of "money matters." This idea is informed by the work we have done over the years. We look for family stories, premises, and language that might indicate long-held ideas about money. This idea emanates from narrative/social constructivist concepts. It aligns naturally with our thought process of exploring family money stories. Again, are there any reasons why women should not understand the family finances? Or if the woman is the primary breadwinner, why does she believe the "administration" of their family finances should be handled by the man? The idea that money is the domain of men is socially constructed and requires questioning. Family finances, just like parenting principles, should be the shared domain of both partners. Roles and responsibilities should be divided practically.

Class

The exploration of socioeconomic class also underpins our workshop. For instance, in the workshop, we encourage participants to examine the thread of class in their family's life, both to see how it has informed their identity and behavior, and to see the effects of any change in class by the family overall or by any individuals within it. Generally, we think of class as a grouping of people based on their similar social factors, including wealth, income, education, and occupation. These factors affect how much power a person has. Class can be understood objectively or subjectively. We focus on an objective view of class and examine phenomena such as what we call "class jumps" or marriages of mixed class.

When we talk about class, we mean two things. First, class is an indicator of resources and proximity to power. By resources we mean education, wealth, income, occupational prestige, as well as someone's parents' education, wealth, income, and occupational prestige. Then, and this is critically important, we also agree with the social psychologists that, "Social class reflects individuals mental representations-of who they are, how they should relate to others, and what they should be doing . . . (leading), in turn, to specific patterns of action and cognition." In other words, while class is a description of a person's outward circumstances, those outward circumstances *create an inner psychological landscape.*

Ideas about class might change when there are major shifts in financial status, such as someone completing advanced education (perhaps for the first time in their family), job loss, death, illness, inheritance, job benefits, or some other major event in a family's life. These moments are usually significant turning points. In our workshops, we explore how families are affected by these status changes and how a person's internal life has adapted to that change. Often, we find that their internal landscape has not caught up to their outer landscape, even though their circumstances changed a long time ago. We also consider the interpersonal dynamics of these moments and how those dynamics affect relationships in the past and present and, ultimately, how they might have aided in constructing premises around money.

We base our work on an amalgam of the above ideas. We both use the framework of family systems as the basis for our work. We believe that the transmission of ideas around money is passed from one generation to the next. Our overall orientation is to honor the complexity of each participant's family and the familial elements that might be brought forward through the workshop process.

Facilitation and Change

Our clinical practice, as distinct from the theoretical, reflects the way we engage with the participants and explore their stories with them. We make the distinction here because we want to highlight the approach we have with all participants. We operate from a collaborative stance. We often share our own issues around money. We look for contextual understanding. We strive to help people come to a conscious and more complex understanding of themselves. And we seek compassion throughout. These concepts form the foundational basis of our facilitation process. Our facilitation goal becomes change.

Change might happen quickly, but, as clinicians, we know that internal change requires time as well as critical consciousness. When we use the term "change," we mean being aware of oneself coupled with the ability to observe oneself critically without judgment, leading to processing the specific issue with its past and present meaning. Ultimately, change occurs over time as we shift from older premises to more current and relevant ones. For our purpose, this difference probably reflects the meaning we apply to change in this context. We look for our participants to begin to think, act or feel differently when dealing with money. We look for participants to be able to take what they discover in the workshop and either alter or modify a specific idea or action around money. This consciousness leads to behavior change, as reported in the feedback from workshop participants. Below are stories from three people who made conscious changes around money issues after taking the workshop. We know about these because of the follow-up conversations we did during the initial stage. These three women reported the change they each experienced after participating in the workshop. This came from follow up conversations we had.

> *Caitlin decided to become more knowledgeable about family finances after participating in our workshop and started looking for financial advisers. For many years, she had depended on her husband to do everything financial. In the workshop, she realized that he may not always be able to manage their finances and concluded that it was her responsibility to become more knowledgeable about their finances. She discussed this with her husband, and they came up with a plan for her to meet with financial advisers to understand more thoroughly what assets they had and what options there were for managing them.*
>
> *Helen decided to purchase a gift for herself, something she had always wanted but would not allow herself to splurge on. During the workshop, she referenced an old family value of "we do not indulge" and started to weigh that against her idea of giving herself a gift. This was the beginning of her change process.*
>
> *Rachel decided to take the leap and leave her job to build up her private practice, a step she had long been reluctant to take. She was able to collaborate with a colleague and map out a financial strategy for transitioning to a full-time practice that would provide substantial*

income. Her initial fear was grounded in financial security through a "paycheck." When she developed a business plan with specific data goals and understood what it would entail to achieve them, she was able to neutralize her fear and move forward on her plan.

As facilitators, we never define what change might look like because change is different for everyone. We know that change in attitude or in one's premises is the first step, with changes in behavior to follow.

For the change process to occur, a person needs to experience critical consciousness, or deeper self-awareness of one's multiple ideas around money. Choosing to come to the workshop itself denotes that a person is conscious of his or her money identity. Although he or she might not be able to articulate precisely why they have chosen to come to the workshop, the format of continuous conversation in relational terms stimulates and brings to the fore that critical consciousness.

Collaboration, Compassion, and Context

As facilitators, our continuous collaborative stance conveys to the group that we are doing this with them, not for them or to them. We do not have the "answers" but rather are facilitating a journey. We engage as a group but do not encourage other participants' interpretation of individual stories. While some group comments might be supportive or enlightening, other comments might be pure curiosity and could derail our facilitation. Our agenda is to have each participant reflect on his or her money identity. If people were to comment on each other, we as facilitators are careful to make sure that the commentary doesn't take over the space. In essence, group collaboration is more about each person participating in his or her individual journey while knowing that others are also participating and having similar issues.

Finally, we encourage compassion for oneself, for each other, and for one's family during workshops to widen one's understanding of a situation.

Meditation

Our workshops are shaped in part by Betsy's meditation practice, which she began twenty years ago after a cancer diagnosis. Betsy began to practice what is called Insight (also called Vipassana) Meditation. Buddhist scholars have been writing about Vipassana Meditation for thousands of years, and it is impossible to convey the complexity of the belief system in a few paragraphs. However, having been influenced by the practice, we believe it is important to give our readers a general sense of the goals and practice.

Insight meditation is the practice of focusing the mind on mindfulness and awakening. The awareness of mental and physical experience allows the practitioner to accept and experience the full range of emotional and physical feelings all humans experience: pain and pleasure, fear and joy, happiness, and sadness. The practitioner becomes accepting of those states of being and does not need to escape them.

Meditation in this tradition means training the mind to silently observe its thoughts. Critically, the goal is to observe the thoughts—but not act on them. This observation and listening are done with compassion and without judgment. As we observe our thoughts, we begin to lose our attachment to them. We begin to see patterns within them. This allows a practitioner to not hide from them, avoid them or be reactive to them. Meditation allows the practitioner to not be controlled by their thoughts. Among the goals of the practice is to see those thoughts and ultimately to distinguish the thoughts from what is real.

Betsy encourages participants in our workshops to observe their thoughts by specifically attending to the precise language of those thoughts. When the language seems outsized or at odds with what is happening, or out of place somehow, that leads to awareness. It allows participants to see that the narrative they attach to something is not necessarily what is real.

We will explain how clinicians can move people toward an awareness of their long-standing narratives about money—a story they are attached to, and within that narrative, a consistent language they use to describe money. That story and that language impact the choices they make. Often money serves as a surrogate for something, or many things, in a person's life. We attempt to unpack all of this.

Facilitated Workshop as Different from Group Therapy

We do not view our workshop as a "group therapy" experience. Group therapy is an ongoing process over a period, where the group repeats relational dynamics that require processing by the facilitator. Our group workshops have different goals. The reason to do this work in a group is to highlight common themes that help to dispel isolation. This makes room for everyone to become more conscious of the meaning of money in their lives. Our workshop is a short-term intervention to facilitate everyone's exploration of their money identity, and we do not focus on how participants relate to each other.

Our workshop is an intense six-hour experience. The focus is for everyone to be reflective and engage in individual exploration. There is limited time for any group dynamic to ensue because the framework is quite defined and paced to keep everyone's process going. The exercises address the theme of money in different ways to allow for the different ways people might process. This results in fostering compassion and conversation, often between the facilitators and the individuals.

Each workshop is comprised of several individuals (6–10 people) who are there to do individual exploration in understanding their money identity to enable change in this sphere of their lives. Paradoxically, it is the fact of multiple individuals doing the same thing which stimulates each individual process, rather than any specific group dynamic that might take place. We work with all these ideas as our theoretical framework in designing and facilitating the workshop. There are somethings we cannot explain explicitly. These are the intuition, flexibility and "being present" that we both bring to the facilitation process. Ultimately, facilitating this workshop has proven to be "an art not a science."

Workshop Design

2

Safe Space

This chapter addresses the question of how to create a workshop space that allows participants to feel safe enough to be vulnerable and explore a taboo subject. When we use the term "safe space," we refer to the structural elements of the workshop, the emotional stimulation and the physically comfortable space that is set up to enable interaction and collective conversation. In focusing on these elements, we try to create an atmosphere that is engaging, non-judgmental, non-threatening, open, inquisitive, collaborative, and physically comfortable.

Participants must feel safe in order to surface vulnerability, which is key for allowing awareness to develop and change to transpire. Some of the factors needed for creating a safe space are structural. This includes limiting the size of the group, thoughtful facilitation, clearly sharing the guidelines of the workshop, meeting for an appropriate length of time, transparently sharing the agenda and timing of the workshop, and ensuring a physically comfortable space. Other factors of a safe space relate to psychological pacing and sequencing. This includes thoughtful consideration of the order of the exercises, the depth of exploration, and amount of sharing we ask of participants. No one is ever coerced to participate or share their thoughts. The fact that no one is "put on the spot" helps everyone maintain control and safety. The exercises move the participants from individual internal silence through sharing with a partner to voluntary group participation. The last hours of the workshop are dedicated to the money-focused genogram, which requires participants to look at the emotional mapping of their family histories around money, work, and class. By the time we reach this section of the workshop, the participants have decreased inhibitions around talking about themselves and are ready to investigate their family money story.

There is no historical precedent that we know of for using a workshop format to address money identity. A great reference that would be useful for facilitating is *The Art of Gathering* by Priya Parker. In this chapter, we will describe how we thought about the structure and the process of the workshop and how we tried to create conditions for participants to feel comfortable being uncomfortable. We know that creating a feeling of safety is crucial for a successful workshop, and we believe that successful workshops can change participants' attitudes and behaviors toward money.

The denouement of the workshop entails each participant creating a money-focused genogram. Because this tool exposes the most personal information about participants' families, it requires vulnerability and trust. It is therefore crucial that we create an environment that promotes comfort and breaks through personal "barriers." While we have used a money-focused genogram tool in one-on-one therapeutic contexts, using this tool in a group environment requires more preparatory trust-building work. Creating a psychologically safe environment for a whole group of people whom we are just meeting for the first time is a challenge that requires forethought and consideration. Importantly, despite the challenges of a group setting, we believe that a group workshop can offer unique benefit. Working in a group on issues of money helps to neutralize feelings of isolation, shame, and mystery surrounding most individuals' money stories. It does the same around preconceived notions about the money stories of others.

During the first stage of our developing the original design/format for the workshop, we focused on membership, space, group interaction, and the co-facilitation process. In the first part of this chapter, we describe the basic ideas of our workshop design. In the second part, we turn toward a discussion of the emotional pacing of the workshop. This is what we have come to understand as the psychological safety created through pacing and sequencing.

Throughout the years of running this workshop, we have sought to maintain a dynamic process by asking for feedback at the end of each workshop. We listen carefully and evaluate how to incorporate the feedback we receive. What we hear mostly is the appreciation for the safe space, the collaborative nature of the experience and ultimately the positive experience of the exposure and exploration of their money identity.

Workshop Design

Number of Participants and Facilitators

We have experimented with finding the right number of participants and facilitators and have concluded that four participants are the minimum with one facilitator, while ten participants are the maximum with two facilitators. Depending on exact circumstances, slight variation is possible in these numbers, but we have found this range to be a helpful rule of thumb. Initially, when we first started testing out this workshop, we set no criteria for participants other than that they be motivated to explore their relationship to money. After running four or five workshops, our beta, we surveyed past participants about changes in their behavior or attitude around money following the workshop. We received quite positive results, noting a high percentage of participants citing change after taking the workshop. Of the

65 percent respondents, 47 percent reported change in either his/her attitude or behavior toward money. There was no specificity of change as we ere just hoping for chane in any area related to money.

This very positive result opened the pathway to offering the workshop on the Ackerman website, which markets mostly to mental health professionals. Because of this placement, most participants who sign up are mental health professionals. We began to see significant opportunities in working with mental health professionals because helping mental health professionals positions them to open conversations about money with their clients. We kept the workshop format and design the same. We added a short piece that stimulates conversation about fees and collection. The objective for this constituency remained the same: exploration of one's money/class identity.

Confidentiality

We believe that it is critical to a feeling of safety to know that everything a person discusses during the workshop is confidential. Asking everyone to accept confidentiality as a condition of the work is the first thing we talk about. We describe the space as confidential and ask that no details of anyone's life get repeated outside of the room. We further enforce the importance of confidentiality by asking everyone to introduce him/herself using first names only. This idea of being in a group of people unknown to you adds another dimension to the "safe space" concept. We have found that most participants feel quite comfortable talking about themselves to people they are just meeting for the first time in our workshop. We believe that starting with a "stranger" lays the groundwork for future conversations with family. By the end of the workshop, participants are often asking to share contacts as comfort and intimacy deepen. This needs to be a unanimous decision and a request that comes from them.

Physical Space

Because the physical space contributes to participants' sense of safety, we gave thought to this matter. What should the room look like? How should people sit? What makes a space feel both personable and professional? After assessing various possibilities, we decided that the workshop is most successful when we start with the participants and facilitators sitting at a long table, mirroring the experience of sitting around a dining room table or a conference table. We chose sitting around a table rather than sitting in a circle of chairs because, in our experience, the table helps people feel less exposed. The table provides participants with a surface to write on, lean on, or use in whatever way they want, giving them a sense of "cover" and sense of safety. The facilitators sit facing each other, allowing them to have a clear view of all participants, as well as each other.

The intention of the group is not to create the kind of group dynamic present in "clinical" group therapy. It is rather for everyone to receive feedback from the facilitators, in addition to moderate input from the other participants, and to surface a diversity of experience. Therefore, the physical set up needs to promote coalescing organically. People do shift seats for the partnership exercises, so the flexibility is important.

Co-Facilitation

We have found that having co-facilitators is extremely helpful. With four eyes and ears watching and listening, we find we catch more of each participant's language, thought patterns, and internal conflicts. Because the workshop's goals are determined by each participant and vary from person to person, the facilitators' sole objective is to empower participants to move in the direction of whatever goals they have set. Given that the end goal is not fixed and universal, the relationship between the two facilitators requires forethought and planning of who will be facilitating which exercise and ensuring that any interventions be done respectfully. Additionally, debriefing each workshop experience together is recommended. Continuous and regular reflection on their dynamic is a requirement. Discussion of the interaction that presents hurdles for both entails that both feel safe and invested and have basic relational comfort for both. Ultimately, the co-facilitators relationship matters for the group to work. Any tension in the facilitator's relationship will affect the workshop process and participants will be distracted and detoured in their own process.

We attribute our co-facilitation success to our commitment to the above principles of the process. We are very specific about the agenda and who will be leading which exercise. We are transparent with the group when we intervene or interrupt. We do all of this respectfully. We are quite diligent about debriefing after each session, both about the participants, as well as about our interaction and dynamic during the workshop. We are not afraid to share with participants when we hold different perspectives about something happening in the room or what someone has said. We find that our differing views are not discomforting but actually serve to model flexibility, curiosity, and our own comfort with expansive non-binary thinking. When we share our different perspectives with the group, we often find that it widens the lens for everyone. We have different professional disciplines. We have generational differences. These issues are not a hindrance. What matters most is that our relationship is founded upon trust, respect, and mutual care, as well as a clear understanding of our shared goal. This is important because facilitation is an art, not a science—and co-facilitation even more so!

Psychological Pacing and Sequencing

We believe that the sequencing of the interactive exercises allows participants to move into a deeper exploration of money and meaning with curiosity and self-reflection. Within the workshop, our goal for each participant is to engage in a money-focused genogram with curiosity and comfort. The sequencing of these exercises entails moving from individual work to a partnered exercise to group conversation. This promotes a deepening understanding of the self and varying perspectives about money. Our pacing from one exercise to the next is key as well to keeping the conversation going and for not getting diverted while still making space for deepening each participant's exploration. Below, we describe the exercises in each of the first two stages of the workshop, which will be described more fully in Chapters 3 and 4. The third stage, the money-focused genogram, will be described in Chapter 6.

Stage One

As each participant arrives, we introduce ourselves and welcome them. Other than small talk about the weather or traffic, we avoid any deeper engagement. We begin with what we call a "hot start" exercise. Betsy asks each participant to fill in the following prompt: "My mom/dad/grandparents used to say . . . about money." She asks them to take a moment to think, write down their responses, and then put them aside. We begin with this opening exercise to help participants begin thinking, even most basically, about their relationship to money. In also centers the transmission in the family context, we follow this activity with introductions. Judy asks each person to share their first name only, what they do professionally, and why they chose to attend the workshop. She is usually the last to introduce herself and does so by mostly describing her professional resume. These first two exercises—the hot start and introduction—serve to bring money "front and center" for everyone. Our third and last exercise in this section involves pairing off the participants and giving them four questions to reflect on connected to money and relationships. We ask them to engage in a discussion with each other, noting that we will ask each partner to introduce his or her partner to the group following their conversation. We ask each partner to take fifteen minutes to respond to the discussion questions before switching. The chatter in the room elevates, and the journey for each person begins. We follow with Judy then asking each person to introduce his or her partner to the group using a "money" lens. This third exercise helps foster a feeling of safety for participants when talking about money and family. This is because the exercise gives participants perspective since they are telling someone else's money story. Often, these partner introductions reveal similar patterns among several participants, helping lessen some participants' feeling of "being alone." We comment on key issues in their stories and, at the same time, maintain the pacing of the reporting. We're always balancing the individual reporting with the tension of our time constraint.

Stage Two

This second stage begins with Betsy guiding participants through an exercise we call "the small money exercise." We have participants focus on a decision they struggled with overspending a very small amount of money, whatever that means to them. The primary goal is to isolate for people the way they talk to themselves about money, the narratives that they have attached to money even when it's a meaningless expenditure. The secondary goal is to surface each person's internal conflict by pursuing the language they use when deciding how to spend money, even an amount of money they would not notice spending. The voice in their head that tells them it's okay and the voice that says it is not. Listening to those voices and that language allows participants to witness and then discuss persistent narratives they project onto money even when it obviously does not make sense. Often people recognize the narrative and the specific words they repeat to themselves, having heard them from their parents or grandparents, or from another source. Connecting the words to the source and seeing how out of place they are in the present circumstance allows people to work toward their own autonomy, addressing what is present in front of them, rather than what they carry from their past.

This second stage moves into identifying money tension points, awareness, and tools to use. Betsy begins by guiding people through a "small money decision" exercise. It is a mindfulness exercise with focus on the simplest money conflict that conjures up voices in our heads. There is a full description in Chapter 4. The goal is to unpack people's dilemmas by constantly pursuing the language of conflict around an insignificant expense. Surfacing conflict entails giving voice to each side of the argument in our heads and noting the precise language our minds use. During this exercise, we do not come to any conclusion. We simply note the language we use to describe the conflict and move on. At this juncture, our goal is to allow the thoughts and feelings that are surfacing to keep coming to the forefront.

Our next two exercises use concepts from Judy's book, *Money and Meaning: New Ways to Talk about Money*, to focus on using values as a language to talk about money. Here we introduce this new idea for how to think and talk about money. Using a card sort exercise developed during the initial research on money and family, the first exercise brings awareness to participants of their core values. A fuller explanation is given in Chapter 5. Its goal is to reveal how we all hold a set of values and yet are not always aware of how those values impact our behavior. The exercise demonstrates how values can be a language to think and talk about money. During the group debrief of this exercise, I often introduce a relational element by asking participants if a spouse or a sibling or a parent were asked to choose cards, would they choose what the individual had chosen. This question introduces the relational element to our conversation and helps participants think about how our values exist in the context of our relationships.

The second values card sort exercise focuses on a big financial decision that participants have made. When we ask what values informed that decision, there is often nonalignment between the values participants list and the core values identified initially. The juxtaposition of these two exercises demonstrates that there are often contradictions in our financial decision-making between what we articulate as our ideals and how we make financial decisions. We give people "permission" to hold these discrepancies but suggest the key to greater functional relationships is to talk about them. In other words, the goal of these exercises is to help participants recognize whether their money decisions and values are aligned or not. We think that talking about any discrepancies is important when cultivating a healthy attitude toward money. These values exercises are a good tool to provide a language for money conversations that can often then reflect an unspoken meaning. It has proven to be a helpful tool for having the money conversations that people too often avoid.

Our last exercise in Stage II uses short vignettes to present specific money issues. We do not offer too much detail but present a case or a situation that requires thought about how to proceed relationally. This exercise highlights the relational dimension that is so often ignored in financial decision-making. It usually brings up the therapists' discomfort with discussing money directly.

These sets of exercises aim to help participants deepen their understanding of the role of money in their lives and understand how money affects their relationships. Becoming aware of the place of money in one's life is the first step in changing one's attitude toward money. These exercises help build toward the money-focused genogram exercise described later. By tuning into our own discrepancies around money, becoming more mindful of, and recognizing money's relational significance, participants can deepen their understanding of the role of money in their lives.

Section Two

Interactive Exercises: A Step-by-Step Description

From Defensiveness to Curiosity

3

In one of our earliest workshops, eight women gathered at a large table in one of the conference rooms at Ackerman, coffee in hand, looking shy but eager. Unfortunately, the workshop booklets we always hand out would not print properly, and Judy had to leave the room to tend to them. It was fifteen minutes before she returned and we could start. As soon as we started, we sensed that our group was becoming more reserved and turned inward; they were making less eye contact and smiling less. We realized that those fifteen minutes of sitting together but not starting the work had had a significant and negative effect on the group, especially on Jane, a participant who worked as a therapist in private practice. As was our usual practice, we contacted participants for feedback after the workshop. When we asked Jane about her experience in those moments, she became agitated and said, "the beginning of the workshop felt chaotic to me, and it made me feel unsafe. I had already walked in nervous." We came to understand that the fear and trepidation participants brought with them into the room grew between when our participants arrived and the time we got started, leading many of them to shut down. Due to this, we shifted the start of the workshop, dropping our traditional introductions and jumping immediately into what we call a "hot" start to take advantage of the momentum people bring by arriving at the workshop and to avoid the opportunity for anxiety to build.

Introduction

Because participants often arrive at the workshop with feelings of trepidation and anxiety, we have come to understand the importance of using the very first moments of the workshop to get our participants immediately and actively reflecting on themselves and their relationship to money. It is critical to establish right away for them to feel safe taking the emotional risk of talking about money. We do this by having them dive into money right away using our "hot start," before conventional introductions or discussing goals. The hot start is a writing prompt. By immediately asking them to engage directly with money and do something active rather than passively listening to instructors or each other, they can experience what it feels like to engage in this taboo discussion and the relief that comes from safely talking about money.

We came to this choice to use a "hot start" after seeing how anxious and shut down our participants were at the beginning of our early workshops. Some participants would appear quiet, cool, tight, or behave shyly or appear closed off. Participants have told us after the fact that they had walked in with trepidation and self-judgment, feeling that talking about money was a transgression against their families' privacy, the rules they had implicitly agreed to with their partners, and broader cultural and social norms. We found that the more time we had before beginning the work, the more we allowed participants' reluctance to build. The more time they had, the more they could retreat into a rigid attachment to their current narrative. We decided that we needed to build emotional and physical safety as immediately as possible so that our participants could begin the workshop from a place of curiosity rather than defensiveness.

To do this, we make sure that as new participants walk into the room, we are warm and welcoming. We convey—explicitly and implicitly—that we are not judgmental and that our sole goal for each participant is to develop their own agency and to increase their ability to talk about and relate to money with neutrality and without emotional charge. This is both a Bowenian theme and a goal we take from a Mindfulness approach. Right from the start, we use warmth and humor to allay their anxiety and to guide them out of a mindset that is "stuck" and into an active and curious mindset. We explicitly tell them that we do not have ideas about what is "right" or "wrong" for them, and we openly encourage participants to stay curious about themselves.

Throughout the workshop, we use a variety of methodologies. In our first phase exercises, we employ writing, self-reflection in pairs, and paired storytelling. Using a variety of methodologies helps keep participants' anxiety at bay and keeps the energy moving. We immediately have everyone actively engaged in an activity—writing—while explicitly telling them that the exercise is for themselves alone, and they will not be asked to share it. The exercises are designed to get them talking—first to themselves through writing and then to each other.

As we stated in our Introduction, our participants' feelings of silence, shame, and isolation surrounding money have historical and cultural roots. Of course, all taboos depend on the context of culture, class, and more, but in this moment in time, discussing the significance and the practicality of money remains a broad American taboo subject. This taboo around money persists even in academic and clinical programs geared toward mental health training mental health professionals, most of which do not teach about working with clients on money-related issues.

In the section that follows, we unpack what we commonly see our participants bring with them into the workshop: secrecy, shame, and isolation around money, which all can block people from opening up. We will further discuss how clinicians can counteract those feelings in order to open the door to deeper work.

Defensiveness and Resistance

When participants walk into our workshop, they are often stuck in a long-standing and dysfunctional narrative about money. Often, they cannot articulate why they signed up and routinely tell us that they are ashamed or embarrassed about how they handle money. They often tell us that they have no one to talk freely with about money. We view this fixed state as psychological resistance.

That resistance is due to internal conflict, which likely stems from one's family of origin. Since most people have been told, whether explicitly or implicitly, that they are not supposed to talk about money, attending a workshop explicitly to discuss money creates conflict. Other sources of conflict may come into play as well, such as a particular societal taboo on women discussing money, which is often thought of as within a male purview. Additionally, people bring forms of conflict that originate in their class background or cultural norms. Someone coming from a poor background, working hard to achieve financial success, or someone coming from an immigrant family, focused on making a class jump, may feel conflict about whether they really "belong" and guilt about leaving their family or community behind. We have also seen internal conflict coming from one's professional background. Artists we have worked with, for example, often feel that talking about money is at odds with their creativity and identity as social outsiders. Many therapists see themselves in a "helping" profession, which they see as counter to money talk.

Our participants walk in carrying a lifetime of conflict and resistance, and so it is essential that we offer them a palpably safe space. We do this in a variety of ways. We smile and greet each person individually, welcoming them as they walk in the door. The first information we deliver is our names and our two rules: that everyone use only their first names and that everyone treat what they hear with total confidentiality. We also make sure to say explicitly that we do not set a goal for them, but instead aim to build their awareness in order to trigger their journey toward discovering what meanings have been attached to money in their conscious and unconscious minds, what stories they tell themselves about money, and how they can claim agency regarding money.

We want to give you a sense of the exercises that we include in the workshop and that have been so effective in allowing participants to explore their lives and identities.

Hot Start

As we discussed earlier, starting one of our first workshops late taught us the importance of beginning quickly and actively. As soon as we start the workshop, we tell everyone that we are going to jump right in and do introductions later. Explaining that this writing will remain private and that we will not ask them to share it, we then ask them to fill in one or more of the following statements:

1. I remember my parents used to say _______ about money.
2. My grandmother always told me ________ about money.

3. I can hear my aunt saying that money was ________.
4. My dad said money _______.

When they finish writing, we tell them to look at the specific words they used in noting the messages they received. We explain that we ask this to show that the words we attach to money are very close to the surface and are very easy to reach. The messages about money and the voices in one's head that attach a narrative to money are right there.

We have found that it is useful to begin with a private exercise because it feels less vulnerable or exposed, and thus entirely safe. We like beginning with a physical activity, writing, rather than asking for "passive" listening. Additionally, by asking participants to think about their families of origin, the exercise immediately connects them to their childhood and their early influences. Lastly, the exercise allows people to tune into and explicitly acknowledge the words and phrases related to money just below the surface, easily accessible, in their minds.

One of our participants, a 60-year-old woman in private practice, Theresa, told us that during the hot start, she heard her father saying, "it's easier to save money than it is to make it." She heard her mother saying to her father, "Miguel, buy something, an apartment, a house, I don't care where, just buy something." And she heard her aunt tell her, "Your mom laughed at your father's jokes until he got funny." While that wasn't explicitly about money, she thought it reflected that her parents had differing levels of confidence in themselves and their futures, and that that may have played out in terms of money as well.

Partner Interview

After jumpstarting the participants' engagement through writing, it is important to begin to counteract their feelings of isolation and to start to foster a sense of community and connection. Feelings of isolation around money are rampant; many people report having never talked about money to anyone outside their partner or family of origin. Many feel that they are the only ones with family money stories, or the only ones who made mistakes with money or who carry conflict about it. Isolation can lead to feeling that "I'm the only one . . ." to feeling ashamed, and to a lack of compassion for the self. Breaking down feelings of isolation is critical for participants gaining perspective.

To do this, we break the group into pairs for a direct and detailed conversation about money. Each partner interviews the other about his or her experience talking about money, which is a first step in breaking through feelings of isolation and shame.

We give each pair the following questions:

1. Do you and your partner talk about money, and, if so, how often? Do you and your best friend? With whom do you talk about money?
2. If you have children, do you talk to them about money, and, if so, in what way? Are there questions they ask that make you uncomfortable?
3. Do you currently talk to your family of origin in the same way about money as you did when you were a child? Are there limits or prohibitions about talking about money within your family?
4. Are there questions about money you want to ask but have not? Why? Is it because you don't know whom to ask or because you have reservations about asking?

We ask them to spend fifteen minutes interviewing their partner using these questions. We caution them to focus on the questions, as we have found that there is often a tendency to avoid discussing money directly and to veer into discussions of emotions and relationships rather than money. We encourage them to help each other stay focused on their interviews about money.

Participants generally jump into this exercise with great animation. We watch them interview each other enthusiastically and openly. They are often surprised by how much they have in common, no matter how different their circumstances. One recent pair practically had to be torn apart from talking when we called time. The young woman stood up to begin introducing her much older male interview partner when she looked at him with surprise and warmth and said, "I feel so close to you but I don't even remember your name!"

The next step is for each partner to introduce the other to the group and tell the other person's "money story." Participants often do so with great compassion and affection, conveying an appreciation of their partner's challenges or accomplishments. They can convey information very neutrally—such as, "Dionne wishes she could speak to her best friend about money but feels she cannot" or "I hear Maribel saying she and her wife talk about money, but her wife does the worrying and she does the reassuring. She wishes they could do more dreaming and planning together." We have literally never heard anyone introduce their interview partner with any hint of judgment, a fact that in and of itself seems to surprise our participants.

There is great power both in telling someone else's story and in hearing our own story told. Whether it is told with warmth, with sympathy, or with simple neutrality, narrating another person's story invites compassion for them, which in turn invites compassion for the self. Importantly, this exercise pulls participants out of a rigid and judgmental approach and into a stance of open curiosity about themselves and their partner. It allows for detachment, the ability to see oneself more objectively, and to analyze the difference between what is real and the stories we tell ourselves. Compassion and detachment taken together help us access our individual money stories, which are founded upon an internal landscape we have built around money, class, and identity.

Counter-intuitively, perhaps, seeing ourselves through someone else's eyes can sometimes help us cultivate self-compassion. To help explain this, we sometimes discuss a story from Betsy's personal life. A close friend was diagnosed with breast cancer in her late 30s. She was prepared to soldier through the treatment, projecting strength, attached to an identity as a strong leader in what was then referred to as the LGBTQ+ community. Because she was a high-profile activist in her city, a newspaper published an article about her going through chemotherapy that included photos of her. When the article came out and she looked at the photos of her, bald and attached to an IV, she told Betsy that she felt a tenderness and compassion for herself in a way that she had not when she was simply in the experience on her own. She softened to herself and gave herself permission not to soldier through, not to feel compelled to behave as a fierce advocate and as an example to her community, not to be attached to her story about being strong. Instead, she said, looking at someone else's picture of herself gave her permission to experience what she was going through fully and authentically.

When Theresa was assigned to conduct the partner interview with Harrison, she wondered how it would go. On the surface, they seemed like quite different people. Harrison had said he was a therapist in private practice who was married to a man "in tech." Theresa was a school social worker at a public school. Interviewing Harrison she realized they had shared experiences in trying to intentionally raise their children with good values. She respected Harrison's determination to raise "decent kids" who would give back, and she felt for Harrison's struggles with one son's addictions and his questions about whether he should support him. When they switched interviewing roles, Theresa shared with Harrison, "I really love my work, but I feel like a terrible mother that I can't provide more for my daughter." She told Harrison that her daughter wants to be an artist. "I talk to my daughter about money all the time," she said, "but I tell her all the time she needs to work—maybe I should have told her to have some fun too." When Harrison introduced Theresa to the group, he talked about how much the two had in common. He said, "I'm so impressed that Theresa has been such a strong example to her daughter not only of hard work but of loving work and choosing work that contributes to the world and that feels purposeful." This was a new framework for Theresa, who thanked Harrison for providing a new way of thinking about her relationship to work, family, and money.

When We Talk to Ourselves About Money

4

Asha is a South-Asian woman in the start-up tech world. Her interview partner who introduces her to the group shares that she is married to a lovely man, a writer who works from home, and that they have three children. She tells us that Asha's middle daughter has an autoimmune disease that makes life challenging physically and emotionally. Asha is open with the group and allows her interview partner to share that she has been very driven in her field and that she makes over a million dollars a year. Her interview partner says that when Asha describes herself, though, she says that she "never thought of herself really as a money-oriented person." She says that she originally thought she might end up working as a teacher and that she "didn't mean to end up in finance." Asha shares that she talks "very comfortably" in her work about money to clients, employees, bankers, and funders. She is very philanthropic and works with several non-profits as well. Asha tells us that she often wonders if she missed her calling and is "supposed to be doing other work." We wonder what has driven Asha toward finance and her focus on money and whether her operating premises about money or narrative about herself and money keeps her from exploring this "other work" that she is drawn to.

Introduction

This section is focused on the question of how practitioners can help people become aware of the narratives and operating premises they hold around money, as well as internal conflicts around money—all of which profoundly influence people's perspectives and drive their behavior. We have found a central belief in Buddhism to be helpful in countering this feeling, and it undergirds the next exercise. This is the idea that human suffering comes from attachment; for our purposes, this means attachment to a story or narrative about money that often operates without our awareness. That attachment to a story keeps us from seeing what is real and in front of us. It blinds us and binds us. Our goal then is to untie those binds, to become aware of the thoughts in our minds, identify the stories we tell ourselves, and free ourselves to see reality apart from story. Like in meditation, in this therapeutic context, detachment is critical for perspective and for changing behavior, and language serves a central role as a source of insight.

In this section, we will describe how clinicians can help participants understand that everyone has a consistent narrative about money—a story they are attached to, within which there is consistent language they use to describe money. That story and that language drive their choices. We will also discuss how money often serves as a surrogate for other things in an individual's life, such that people use money for purposes other than its assigned value.

Awareness

Most participants arrive at our workshop without an understanding that everyone has a specific and persistent narrative about money that is not necessarily based on their reality as much as the messages they received earlier in life. They are also frequently unaware that money has a meaning in their lives beyond its use as a currency for the exchange of goods and services. They do not see how certain patterns of behavior have been influenced by money narratives or how these narratives affect their relationships, including relationships with family members, work colleagues, and friends. These stories about money always operate; they cloud a person's ability to see what is real and unknowingly influence their decisions and behavior.

Our goal for our participants is for them to reclaim their ability to see their financial lives with clarity and to be in control of their behavior and decisions to the greatest extent possible. We refer to this as agency.

To develop agency, we believe our participants are served when they see the narratives at play in their lives and can decide if those narratives serve them or should be let go. We work with participants to identify those stories by tuning in to hear how each individual talks to themselves—the exact words they use—all day long.

The workshop is based on the idea that people have conflicts, shame, guilt, fear, and secrets about money. One way to address this conflict is to isolate it and reduce it to very few, honest words. To do that, we must listen to how we talk to ourselves.

Influenced by meditation techniques, we believe that the mind can learn to observe mental and physical processes and experiences with detachment and compassion. Listening to one's thoughts allows a person to break the hold those thoughts have; listening to our thoughts allows for new insights and the ability to avoid being ruled or controlled by them.

To focus specifically on internal language and narratives around money, we use an exercise called "the Small Money Decision." By focusing on a minor decision, the exercise helps participants notice that they have strong, outsized language attached to extremely minor financial decisions—language that we often see come up later in the workshop in other exercises.

Small Money Decision

By using the "small money decision" exercise, we begin to spark awareness of participants' internal narratives (and internal conflicts). We ask the individuals to think of a recent decision they made that entailed spending money. We tell participants it must be an actual decision that they paused over or struggled with, not a choice they made easily or reflexively. It must be a decision participants made on their own, not in partnership or conversation with another person. Lastly, and most importantly, it must be a decision they made to spend an amount of money so small (whatever "small" means to them) that they would not notice that amount being gone from their wallet.

Decisions our participants have discussed included giving a $1 tip, buying a $2 bottle of water, taking the subway for $3 or a taxi for $8, buying a book that is new or saving $3 buying a used one, buying a $20 gift or $30 gift for a niece, ordering with Instacart or grocery shopping, buying Dunkin Donuts coffee or Starbucks, spending $7 to sit in a coffee shop to get some space from a crying newborn, and buying the "nice" kitchen tile or the "just fine" kitchen tile. Each of these decisions involved, in the eyes of the participant narrating it, a small amount of money.

After participants think of an example, we work to explore the language that bubbled up when they were struggling to make their decision. Betsy will ask them, "What occurred to you when you thought about spending the $2 on the water?" Often the first language participants offer is vague: "I shouldn't spend so much money" or "it's a waste" or "I don't need it" are the frequent "don't spend" thoughts, while thoughts such as "I want it," "I feel like it," or "what the heck, I deserve it" are often the first words offered as the thought that says "spend." We encourage participants to dig deeper and get more specific. Often Betsy prompts participants, asking, "What does the voice say that says to spend the $4? What exactly does the voice that says 'don't spend' say?" Betsy will often explain that while distilling these voices can feel reductive, doing so is useful to ascertain a core, underlying idea.

Returning to Asha, with whom we opened this chapter is instructive for seeing how reckoning with a decision about a small amount of money illuminates core beliefs and tensions around money in a person's life. Asha tells us that her husband has a flexible schedule which allows him to spend time with their children, while she works very long hours. They live a forty-minute ride by public transportation from her work. Every single morning, she debates whether she should spend $22 on a taxi, which would give her twenty extra minutes with her daughter. "When I debate whether or not to take a car service, a lot goes through my head," she explained to the group. "I wonder whether it's too much money. But I also tell myself that the money is worth less to me than it's worth to the cabdriver, given the cost of living in my city. And then I remind myself how much I make at work and that I can afford it. I work such long hours and 20 minutes means a lot to me and my girl." Betsy prompts Asha to pay attention to the specific voices in her head during these moments of decision. "The voice that tells me not to take the taxi says I'm *irresponsible*. Over and over that's what I hear," she explains, making a face that indicates that it feels like an odd word to use for what is for her such a small amount of money. It is powerful for participants to hear these words spoken out loud. The exercise in this case has allowed some of the language that is controlling her to surface. We do not yet know the origin of that language, what the story is behind it, or what "responsible" and "irresponsible" mean to Asha—questions that will be explored in the rest of the workshop.

Identifying the simplest form of the language below the surface that we attach to decisions often reveals a fundamental conflict. This language identification allows our participants to observe when the narratives they attach to money are out of place or overblown for the circumstances. A participant, for example told us that buying the better theater tickets that cost $10 more felt "selfish." One participant said that if she bought three books for her young cousin, everyone would think she is "showing off," but if she bought only two books, it would seem "unloving." One woman told us "if I pay retail for that sweater, I'm not my mother's daughter," another that if she bought herself a pair of earrings "she might run out of money or end up homeless." The words people use—"take advantage," "selfish," "unloving"—can seem absurd in the context of such a small decision. But noticing that absurdity and strangeness can be useful, drawing participants' attention to previously unexamined assumptions and helping them examine their relationship to money with detachment and curiosity.

By fostering awareness and compassion for the self, this exercise supports participants' agency. The work of fostering agency requires time to process. We deliberately do no further analysis or exploration as part of this exercise. We allow the language that participants note to stand on its own and to simmer, noting only that we will all watch out for the words and phrases that have surfaced to reappear in other activities.

While we believe this work is useful one-on-one in a therapeutic setting, it is perhaps even more powerful in a group where one by one each person recognizes themselves in their fellow participants' stories. It is often the exercise that gets people laughing the most as they feel relieved from their loneliness and hear themselves telling something that they live with all day every day but see as absurd.

Over time, we have seen that certain patterns and categories of language and narrative emerge as part of this exercise. We often see, for example, language that describes safety, survival, and danger. Sometimes language relates to gender or culture or class or to very specific circumstances in a participant's family of origin. One participant, for example, shared that she spent two hours scouring the internet to save $8 because she "didn't want anyone to take advantage of [her]." We found out later that that aphorism was something she learned from her parents and that they learned as a truism from their parent who had survived the Holocaust by not allowing anyone to take advantage of them. It always seems outsized for the size of the money it is describing, and there is always a conflict. And that is our point. People are thinking about money all the time, using language that is often not actually theirs, language that has weight and meaning they do not usually examine, and language on two sides of an argument. In other words, there is often conflict. As one of our participants said recently "money is everywhere, and nowhere!"

We learned a great deal about Asha during her genogram. She told us that her parents both worked—her mother quite consistently as a translator, her father very sporadically. He alternated between fantastic success, having enormously productive periods of time when he would make a lot of money, and the family would live very well. Then it would come crashing down. He would lose his job, and it would take a long time until he could find new work. Asha never knew why this was. During times when he did not work, her mother's family would take them in. We asked her what the narrative was about his ups and downs. She told us that she looks back on the experience now as an adult and believes that her father had productive periods and severely depressive periods. We ask her how this was discussed when she was a child. She tells us: my mom's parents would say "he's irresponsible." We remind her that this was the language she used when describing taking a car service. She recognizes that and remarks, "yeah, I guess in some way every time I spend money I'm wondering if I'm acting like my father, checking if I'm depressed and headed for ruin." We ask her if she understands her choice to go into finance rather than teaching in a different way now and she nods and says she does. We ask what her new understanding is and she replies, "I think it made me feel safe financially in a way I didn't feel as a child, and I also found it reassuring that I was productive and consistently making money because to me that means I'm emotionally stable."

Values
Making the Invisible Visible

5

Ann, a 40-year-old white woman, manages a sex therapy practice group in Chicago. The practice includes five therapists. When she introduced herself to the workshop group, she highlighted her struggle with talking to clients about fees. She told us that she strongly believes that people should not need to pay for help. She could not align this belief with her setting a fee schedule. We wondered how she would respond to our Values Exercise and if the exercise would help her clarify the distinction between her clients' need for help and her business sustainability. We noted the tension between these two competing values. We questioned how this "belief" of clients not having to pay, if implemented, might affect operating a group practice that was supporting five therapists.

This chapter focuses on how to help people identify and explore their values, thereby gaining an important tool for talking about money with greater ease and agency. Values, in this exercise, are a language that can be used to talk about money. We use a card sort exercise that helps people identify and choose what their values are today. This exercise was developed as part of the Money and Family Life Research Project that Judy started and has directed for two decades at the Ackerman Institute. That research project demonstrated that money is still a taboo subject for most families, leading those researchers to develop this card sort methodology to help families engage in conversations about money. What often surfaces in the debrief process is the tension between two or more competing values. The purpose of surfacing these tensions is to bring depth of understanding to communication around money and provide a language for broader definition. Tensions are often present and often ignored or denied. Acknowledging their existence and using values to talk about them often leads to more productive conversations.

In 2000, Judy put together an interdisciplinary group to look at the work she and others had done in family business consulting in order to explore and develop tools for better family functioning around the issue of money. The members of the research team represented multiple perspectives in a family business: Some members had been part of a family business, others had worked professionally with family businesses, and a few were family therapists who had worked with families with family businesses. After months of discussion, the project team developed two different values card sorts to break the taboo of discussing money in families. One is focused on content values and the other represents process values. Content values refer to concrete issues, such as education, integrity, and work, while "process values" refer to the way things are done, whether collaboratively, hierarchically, transparently, or secretively. We tested these exercises out with multiple diverse groups of people and families to discover that the exercises could be used with universal population. Linking money and values using these card sorts proved to be effective in opening money conversations and getting families to think and talk about money differently.

In facilitating these exercises, we have found that most people are not fully conscious of their own values. We believe that with greater awareness of one's values comes a greater sense of self-determination, as well as a language to use in money conversations. For this exercise in the workshop, we use the content card sort only, as we do not have enough time in the day to use both. Our objective is to introduce participants to using values as a way of communicating about money and their own priorities and choices when it comes to financial decisions.

The workshop's initial exercises, as described in chapters three and four, raise the consciousness of money and meaning for the individual participant. In this next set of exercises, beginning with the card sort exercise, we offer participants a value-based discourse as a language to talk about money and money-related decisions. The card sort technique is particularly useful for this because it helps participants visually identify and sort values and distinguish between them, rather than remaining in the realm of abstract discussions. It also helps them differentiate between those values that are most important to them at their particular stage of life. The actual process is explained later in this chapter. It is effective in providing a clear description and a way to prioritize and make distinctions. This exercise affords an alternative communication tool because values are a less intimidating conversation than money and not socially prohibitive in the same way. Money has so many varied emotional connections like shame, jealousy, guilt, gratitude, and power. These multiple meanings are often unrecognized and buried because of the tension they might create for an individual. As a result, the conversations are avoided. When people shift to discussing money through the lens of values, it becomes less prohibitive.

It moves those involved to view conversations about money from the individual to the interpersonal perspective, introducing a new idea about how values can be used for more constructive conversations It allows people to view others' choices more generously, since, even if one disagrees with someone else's money decision, they can see that it comes from a positive value. It allows for hearing a different perspective. It shifts the tenor of the conversation because new meaning has been added. As a result, the conversation between family members becomes more expansive and informative.

This exercise also helps participants practice how to manage conversations without eruption. It also moves people to develop confidence in their own agency around money. When a person can discern for him/herself the clear understanding of value priorities relating to money choices, they develop faith in their ability to handle money. These shifts lead to fruitful conversations that are crucial for bettering familial dynamics. By eliminating mysteries around money, and enabling constructive conversations, we promote healthier family functioning.

Value: Moving Core Values to a Conscious Level

In our experience, most people cannot easily name their own core values. When prodded, they might come up with one or two values, but usually not more than that. From a young age, most of us pick up core beliefs that become ingrained. We might change these values over time, but even that does not mean that we are aware of our values. This exercise encourages participants to consciously name their current core beliefs and values. In short, consciousness of one's belief system is the essence of this exercise.

We use a small card deck made up of fourteen cards, each of which has a value written on it, such as "relational," "educational," "work," "financial," "material," and more. Below the "headline" word, we include three bullet points that might be used to describe that particular value. The bullet points are there to stimulate participants' thoughts about what that value might mean for them. Over the course of the Workshop we began to offer participants a blank card so that they had the opportunity to add any values they felt strongly about but which were not represented by the exisiting cards. These cards can be seen in the template at the end of this chapter.

Judy introduces this exercise. She divides the instructions into two steps. For the first step, she asks the participants to divide the cards into two piles: those that represent values that are more important to them and those that are less important, explaining that we are often not conscious of how values inform our behavior and acknowledging that values are not stagnant and shift over time. After these points of clarification, she reiterates the instructions to choose those values that are important or unimportant in one's present stage of life. Participants often respond to these instructions with questions such as, "how we are now or what we aspire to be?" "this is so hard," or "how many cards in each pile?"

She responds graciously, as these questions reflect the difficulty of the exercise for participants due to their lack of consciousness/ awareness of their own values, as well as their underlying unease with the topic. Those who are aware of their own beliefs and values are likely to engage in the activity with more fluidity and ease. Given the difficulty most people have with the exercise, however, it seems to us that most people are not "in tune" with their own beliefs.

To illustrate some of the responses to this first stage of the exercise, I return to Ann, the psychotherapist who stated that her clients should get what they need, regardless of their ability to pay. During this exercise, she kept staring at the fourteen cards in front of her. She spent time moving them around, deep in thought. She had difficulty creating two piles of cards, and Judy encouraged her to think about her life today and which cards would describe her life most accurately. She continued to adjust her choices, though, and eventually was able to create the two piles.

Judy then explains the second step of the exercise, introducing the concept of "core values," as distinct from situational values. She suggests that we all have four or five values that are always reflected in our behavior and thoughts, whether we are with a partner, colleague, friend, or other family member. She asks participants to choose the top four or five values from the pile of cards that are important to them. These are the basic values that inform who we are, what we think, how we perceive ourselves, and how we act.

There are usually very few questions, and our participants are typically able to complete this step easily. Judy then asks the participants to write down the values they have chosen and asks each participant to share those values with the group, along with a reflection on whether the choice was difficult for them and, if so, what created the hurdle.

Returning to Ann, she notably listed her four core values with ease: "relational," "philanthropic," "ethical," and "work." She then shared with the group her dilemma in the first step: Some of the cards had "overlap" for her. For example, she wasn't sure of the difference between "philanthropic" and "public value." She finally settled on philanthropic because of her belief about whether people in need should have to "pay for service." This led to a discussion about how she had set up her clinic practice as a "not-for-profit." Judy queried her about her way of funding the practice and its sustainability. Ann emphatically stated that the practice had to be philanthropy and not a business. Judy concluded on a general note about not-for-profit organizations, explaining that an organization, whether it is "for profit" or "not-for-profit," must have resources to pay for overhead and salaries. Ann initially looked quizzical but then understood the point Judy was making. Ann articulated a new understanding that charging her clients enabled her to do her work and mused about the possibility of using a sliding scale to give her clients the help they needed. The exercise pushed Ann to be more discerning about her core beliefs, leading to practical and helpful new orientations and behaviors that would reflect these values more effectively.

As we go around asking each person to share and reflect on the experience, Judy introduces a relational element. She asks, "If your spouse were in the room and I gave them these cards and asked them to choose the four or five cards that best describe you, what would they choose?" She might also ask about what someone's parents or siblings might choose for them. This line of questioning produces a range of responses and surfaces the question of "how well known" am I with by family?" This line of questioning is important because it introduces a relational lens, which is crucial for participants to use when understanding their own money identity. Interpersonal relationships very often effect our money, whether in our families of origin or by a partner or spouse. Using a relational lens surfaces these complexities and helps transition the workshop from focusing on the individual to focusing on the relational and interpersonal.

It is instructive to again return to Ann to understand the impact of this relational element. After Ann shared her core values with the group, Judy asked her what values her fiancé would choose to describe her, and she responded that he would probably choose three of the five values that she had chosen. Judy then asked what other two he might have chosen that she had not. She was surprised that she said "financial" and "recreational." Betsy pointed to the interesting difference and wondered how Ann understood it. This again opened up further conversation about Ann's original dilemma and her struggle with aligning her values and her work. Importantly, although either of us may probe a particular comment or pursue a line of discussion that we believe will lead to further explanation, we also both leave space for the participant to process the information and avoid prescriptive declarations. The probing/questioning that we do, stimulates the participants' exploration and reflection on their money story more discerningly.

Financial Decision-Making and Values

The second exercise using the card sort is about making a big financial decision. It presents the concept of contradiction. Inevitably, there is not an exact alignment between the personal values in the first exercise and those in this second one that inform the financial decision. Judy starts by asking participants to think about the last big financial decision they made, such as refinancing a mortgage, taking a vacation, buying a car, or deciding to pursue a graduate degree. She asks them to shuffle the cards and then choose the four or five values that informed their decision-making. Generally, most participants do this quickly. Again, Judy goes around, asking participants to share their decisions and the values they chose. She then asks them to look back at their core values, which everyone had written down. About half of the time, there are discrepancies between the core values chosen in the first exercise and those values chosen as informing their financial decision. The point of this exercise is to highlight that our financial decisions are not always in alignment with our core values, which demonstrates the tension between what we think and say, on the one hand, and what we do in practice, on the other. We need to know if and when this discrepancy exists and acknowledge that to those around us, perhaps using the values as a way to explain our actions. Doing this sets the stage for more transparent and productive discussions for everyone.

This exercise helps give participants the tools for more expansive conversations around money and financial decisions. Making participants' own conflicting feelings and values more transparent allows for greater understanding among couples, parents and children, or business partners. If and when we have an expanded understanding of someone's thoughts, it can change our perspective and shift our position. When one can be more discerning about an issue and understand their own relationship to a given set of values, it helps one to better articulate their own motivation in a decision or the meaning they attach to it. This deeper understanding may lead participants to make different choices, or it may simply make them more comfortable with agreeing to disagree while avoiding conflict because those involved better understand each other.

After this exercise, Ann took a deep breath and shared with the group the relief she felt. She and her fiancé had talked incessantly about her setting up her practice as a "not-for-profit." She had never had the language to explain her dilemmas and thought process. She was looking forward to discussing it now that she had a better way to explain her feelings to her future husband. She added that she also understood what he had been trying to say to her. She was looking forward to the conversation.

Evelyn is a Black woman who works as a psychologist at her children's school. Evelyn's interview partner tells us that she grew up lower working class. She says that her family either fought about money or was silent about it. All she remembers being told by her parents was "we're poor, we'll always be poor." She wants her life and her children's lives to be different. She talks very practically to her children about money. In fact, she tells the story of her 9-year-old daughter who asked a boy she had a crush on what his credit score was! Evelyn has worked hard to develop a second job as a therapist, and she now charges private clients $125/hour. She is financially stable and even able to make plans for buying a house, taking vacations, and having a future with creature comforts. Evelyn tells us she is participating in the workshop because she had started to wonder if she should give up her steady school job and spend her energy building her private practice, which could be more lucrative but was of course not guaranteed to work out. A close friend of Evelyn's has become very well known, a celebrity with a huge following on social media. The friend is encouraging her to expand her Instagram presence so that the friend can send her clients and she "can make some real money." Quitting her school job and focusing exclusively on private clients would make her much more money, but she is concerned that she might have difficulty maintaining her professionalism with this potential new clientele because of the class difference she might feel with them. We suggest to Evelyn that using the values exercise might be a good tool for her to think about herself and her clients and to understand where there might be real differences.

Table 5.1

Personal Values • modesty • loyalty • faithfulness	Philanthropic Values • contribution of time • and money • to care for others
Economic Values • financial responsibility • maximizing profit • frugality	Financial Values • financial independence • preservation of wealth • stewardship
Ethical Values • integrity • justice • fairness	Public Values • good citizenship • community involvement • government service
Physical Values • health • relaxation • quiet time alone • exercise	Recreational Values • sports • leisure activity • hobbies • family vacations
Spiritual Values • inner spirituality • faith • religious commitments	Material Value • possessions • life style • social standing
Relational Values • family • friends • work associates	Work Values • professional achievement • competence • stewardship
Cultural Values • music • visual arts • travel	Educational Values • study • self-improvement • academic achievement

Money-Focused Genogram

6

Throughout the day, Jean, a psychotherapist, had been attentive and reflective. When we got to the part of the workshop where we create genograms, Jean expressed excitement, explaining that she was hoping for some insights about her family's money history and that she felt ideas had been "bubbling up" since the morning. We had learned a bit about Jean during the partner conversation exercise. She had worked as a social worker in a school setting, and she and her husband talked a lot about finances and had done financial planning. In addition, she shared with the group that she and her siblings were helping her parents financially, and her interview partner had noted there were tensions between her and her aging parents around money. Following her partner's introduction, Judy had asked Jean if she wanted to share any details, and Jean had said that she preferred to wait. Now Jean was ready to talk about the tension with her aging parents using the genogram.

This chapter focuses on how to facilitate a money-focused genogram most productively within a small group workshop.

A genogram is a graphic picture of family history and patterns showing the basic structure, demographics, functioning, and relationships over three generations of a family. These are simple, pictorial representations used to elicit information and track stressors and resources. Perhaps their most effective application is being able to detect patterns. They provide an emotional map of family relationships, highlighting recurring themes within a family's history, as well as a timeline of significant events, such as births, deaths, marriages, divorces, and illnesses.

Monica McGoldrick and Randy Gerson developed the genogram tool in 1985, based on principles developed as part of Murray Bowen's theoretical framework in his *Family Therapy in Clinical Practice*. By collaboratively creating a genogram together, professionals and clients can explore family relationships and the repercussions and influences of generational transmission of different beliefs and circumstances. Genograms often produce an "aha" moment that clarifies a client's family dynamics, and they can be used as a short-term tool, as we do in the workshop, or long-term over the course of treatment, in which case new information is continuously added to the genogram.

In the workshop, we create a genogram focused on work, money, and class. We narrow the scope of the genogram to accommodate time, information, and reflection.

Genograms are not commonly used in group settings, and we have, in fact, never heard of it being used in a group setting that is a workshop rather than a therapeutic environment. We say this because a workshop is a singular event and a genogram shows the emotional dimension of one's family, an intimate picture. Although it is impossible to prove, we believe that our workshop is the first time genograms have been used in a group setting of strangers. We reiterate this to convey to our readers the sensitivity that this requires.

We designed our workshop with a money-focused genogram as its centerpiece to understand its efficacy as a tool in impacting the change process for our workshop participants. We chose it because it notes historical change and context over the lifetime of a family. This graphic helps to stimulate change, whether in attitude or behavior, in participants' money identity.

Roadmap

In this chapter, we will show how to use a money-focused genogram. In our workshops, we begin by having participants simply map the members of their family. We then present questions that elicit content about work, money, and class dynamics and histories in the family. We explore the impact on family relationships. We consider the family's social and cultural context as well.

We aim to stay focused on the themes of money, work, and class because these areas are most fruitful for probing the interface between money and family. The goal is for individuals to begin to see visually the story, themes, or patterns of emotional dynamics that become apparent. Sometimes the group's questions can become a distraction or a detour from an issue that might not be relevant. The facilitator has to use his/her skill to manage this process. As a result, the facilitator's role is threefold: to observe the information that emerges; to reflect on the patterns as they are revealed; and to maintain the role of primary conductor of the genogram process. The genogram is a collaborative journey, and so facilitators should take an inquisitive stance to promote the best results.

Set Up for the Exercise

When we started doing these workshops, Judy would facilitate each participant's genogram. This process took more time than we had and required each participant to sit through and observe all the other participants' genograms. We shifted our method to first demonstrating one genogram to the whole group and then pairing off participants to have them practice creating each other's genograms.

We tell the group that we will ask each participant to present their partner's genogram, as well as to reflect on the experience of mapping their own money, class, and work-related family history. Throughout the process of partnering and the presentation, the facilitators must manage both the group and individual participation, maintaining the focus on tracing money, class, and work in the family. (Other factors like culture may also be pursued more deeply where relevant.) The facilitators must also help ensure that participants do not detour too far from the central focus, which is a common problem. The facilitators connect themes, material, and language that surface in the presentation of the genogram. We also make connections to what has emerged in previous exercises. This must be done carefully and collaboratively with each participant. Creating a graphic picture and demonstrating patterns and themes, along with questions and connections often leads to significant emotional insights for participants.

Here are the steps we take:

- Start by mapping familial membership and nature of relationships.
- Add socioeconomic standing: social class, cultural, racial, or ethnic background, and immigration status and if/how those have shifted over time.
- Explore the nature of family members' work and the familial meaning of success.
- Explore how money is discussed and how attitudes towards money are expressed.
- We ask about money crises or transitions (divorce, death, illness), and how was money handled in these moments.
- We ask if there were gendered roles around money in the family.
- We ask about the intra-familial relational dynamics around money and work.
- We discuss the role of class within a family's self-understanding.

In fleshing out our understanding of the role of a genogram, it is instructive to look at an example, and so we return to Jean's family. We learn through her genogram that Jean is the oldest child in her family of origin and has two younger siblings, both of whom are married. We learn that she has two adult children, but her siblings do not have children. We also learn that her father's parents were immigrants and that her mother's parents were born in the United States. She tells us that her aging parents were married, divorced, and then remarried each other.

When there is a divorce in a family, it is important to pursue questions about the divorce because divorce is a major stressor for everyone in a family, it is helpful to get a deeper understanding of the process, both emotionally and financially. If there have been other crisis events, such as major health challenges or deaths, that have impacted the family's financial life, the facilitator should pursue these as well.

Given this, we ask Jean a series of questions about the divorce: how and why the divorce happened, how old was she when her parents divorced and when they remarried, and how she and her siblings understand how and why the divorce as well as the remarriage happened. These questions prompt Jean to tell us more about her family's socioeconomic standing. Note that most of the questions that led to this information focus on Jean and the experience as she remembers her perspective of these family events.

Her father was a contractor and her mother a "stay-at-home mom" until Jean was in high school. Until that point, the family never "wanted" for anything and lived a middle-class lifestyle. But then, her family situation began to unravel. The family learned that her father was a gambler and had lost big, forcing him to sell his business to pay his gambling debt. She remembers her mom saying, "At least we still have our home!" Her mother went to work as a manager in a medical office to support the family, and her father had to work for his competitor. Jean recounted how difficult this was for him, and she recalled lots of tension between her parents, including her mother's resentment and her father's shame. The family survived, but it was very challenging for everyone. Jean, a teenager during this period, coped by spending lots of time with her friends away from the anger at home. She also noted how much her father changed and how painful it was to experience his transformation from a thriving, exuberant person to a cowering individual. Eventually, her parents divorced because her mother caught her father gambling again. By that time, Jean was married and somewhat distanced from her parents' drama.

Given the information that surfaced during the reporting of Jean's genogram, it was important for us as facilitators to continue the line of questioning around how money was managed in the family, demonstrating to the group how we deepen the exploration when deemed appropriate.

We therefore asked the following questions:

- How did your parents manage money during your childhood?
- Were there any significant messages that were conveyed about money, either implicitly or explicitly?
- Is there language around money that resonates?
- Were there any significant changes that took place during your time at home?
- What were the premises around money held in the family story?
- Do you manage your finances similarly or differently from how your parents managed money when you were growing up?
- Have you and your siblings ever talked about money management in your family?

We now know that Jean's childhood money experiences were tense and conflictual. Our questions, therefore, try to follow specific threads that might expand her understanding of how her money beliefs developed over the course of her life. She shares with us that her father would bring home the money and give her mother a "family allowance" for bills and household expenses. It is unclear whether Jean's mother had any understanding of the bigger financial picture. Jean shares that it was always a struggle to make ends meet even before her father's business went into bankruptcy, and Jean and her siblings would try to disappear when the time came to pay bills. The constant fighting meant that Jean and her siblings were not shocked by the divorce, and they felt grateful that the fighting would finally come to an end. By the time Jean's parents decided to remarry, Jean and her siblings had been married and out of the family home for some time. Although her parents remarried, they never really addressed their problems around money. In addition, Jean explains that for a long time, she and her siblings tried to get her parents to do financial planning, but to no avail. Jean notes that her parents now have very little money, and their health has deteriorated drastically. They need aids to help them with daily functioning, and this cost has become their children's burden. Jean is torn by her feelings of responsibility, anger, and frustration. Looking at her genogram, she blurts out "What were they thinking?!" She comments on the chaos that erupted in her family because of her father's addiction. There had been so much mystery around the family eruption and so many unanswered questions.

At this point, we have information about the marital dynamic in Jean's family of origin around money and their socioeconomic status. In addition, we have more clarity as to what happened in Jean's childhood and how money was managed (or in this case, not managed). When Jean talks about her parents, one can hear the anger in her voice, which, as a facilitator, Judy mentally notes as an area for further exploration. We also know from Jean's response during the values exercise earlier in the day that financial responsibility is deeply important to her and her husband. Judy notes aloud that Jean has attempted to do nearly everything quite differently from her parents. The question remains, however, about the emotion and anger Jean expressed. Where has that gone? If we were to explore this more deeply with Jean, we might discover that underneath her anger is the shame she felt during her teenage years when her family experienced their economic downturn. Judy shares her hypothesis with Jean and suggests that she consider further exploration. Jean, who is a therapist herself, agrees and thanks Judy for the suggestion.

Often in the workshop, we can touch very vulnerable places for our participants. As we continued our exploration with Jean, Judy realized that this was one of those moments. If she had been alone in her office with Jean, she might have continued with these questions:

- What emotions come up for you around money: fear, guilt, pride, or shame, greed or envy, power or powerlessness?

- Do any emotional reactions relate to actual experiences? If so, can you talk about these experiences?
- Do you think your mother or father feels or felt those same emotions?
- Are there differences between you and your family of origin in handling and talking about money?
- Are there any themes or patterns that you are seeing emerge as we do this?

Had we continued with Jean along these lines of questioning, our guess is she would have come to recognize that her anger masked some deeper feeling of shame that she had experienced during her teenage years. Helping her to process that shame would begin to neutralize her anger and get her to a less conflictual place. This might enable her to decide how to deal with her parents' situation in the present without as much conflict.

Role of Facilitators

As facilitators, we have to walk a fine line between knowing when to dig deeper into our participants' issues and when to hold back. Although this is a delicate dance, having two people facilitate helps us achieve balance. During these more vulnerable moments, it is important for the facilitators to remember that the goals of the workshop are to raise consciousness around money to allow participants to continue the "work" of self-reflection and exploring the multigenerational dynamic of their relationship to money. While the workshop environment is safe, it is not a therapy session, and not every issue that arises can be pursued in its fullness. The workshop is instead meant to be a beginning, with each participant setting out on their own journey exploring their money identity.

We have found that facilitation works best when we remain curious, asking questions and musing over connections that surface for each participant throughout the day's interactive exercises. The most challenging part during this section, following the genogram, is to respect but limit input from the other participants. While the presence of a group is helpful for breaking isolation and developing compassion for the self by exhibiting it toward others, we don't want participants to start playing facilitator or to detour the conversation. The facilitators must ensure that the conversation stays focused on the money and work-related issues and continue to mine personal background information that helps participants gain a deeper understanding of patterns related to money/work or class that surface.

Awareness of these sorts of patterns emerges in a natural way over the course of the workshop. For example, during the "small money" exercise earlier in the day, Jean had talked about her anger when she saw a tip jar at Starbuck's. Betsy had prompted her to uncover the voices in her head that were conflicted. Jean had shared that she was angry that the jar was there and would feel embarrassed if she did not leave something. These two emotions, anger and shame, were the same two that then surfaced during the genogram. Jean looked at us and simply said, "thank you, this has been so helpful. I understand my own shame, and now I wonder about my parents' shame and how I might have absorbed some of that."

Recurring Patterns

When working on an individual genogram, patterns become evident. Over many years of doing these money-focused genograms, there are several patterns and themes that we have seen recur frequently in our work on these questions. One common pattern is for women and men to adopt socially gendered roles in their relationships and specifically in their handling of money. What this means is that women give up their financial responsibility in the service of the relationship. This often means women pay the bills and men make the financial decisions for the family. This assignment of roles leaves the women not knowing significant financial information. Although there may be many reasons for this, we try to promote the concept of "partnership" and everyone's knowledge about family finances in the workshop. We emphasize an important distinction between administering the finances and longer term financial decision-making and promote the idea that joint financial decision-making requires knowledge and transparency, which avoids the problems of relationships and decisions that play out according to gendered roles.

Another theme that often surfaces as we discuss genograms in more depth is a desire to be taken care of by one's partner or parent. This wish for dependency can create a burden for the partner and lead to dysfunctional behavior. If we go back to Jean's parents, we know that, even though her mother administered the money, her father handled all financial decision-making. We do not know why her mother agreed to getting an allowance, and our goal is never to assign blame. But exploring these patterns is important for understanding how and why a dynamic develops into a pattern, which is something participants must be aware of if they wish to change it. Although her parents were not able to manage this dynamic, Jean was able to do so in her partnership, which can also prompt further querying.

A third very common pattern we see when exploring participants' genograms is an inherited feeling of safety or danger regarding money. We find that if a prior generation in a participant's family history overcame danger and found safety with a particular approach to money—whether that be risk-avoidant behavior or high-risk behavior, by working enormously hard or keeping vigilant against anyone attempting to take advantage of them—it is often the case that participants notice, via the genogram, that they themselves are playing out the same behavior because of an underlying, often unconscious belief that doing so will keep them safe, even though the historic danger has entirely passed. It is an outdated adaptive behavior that may no longer serve the person.

In what follows, we will present two short and illustrative vignettes of participants who realized through the genogram the ways in which they were holding onto a particular family idea from their past. Once gaining awareness of this historic shadow and its continued effect, each was able to quickly recognize the lack of alignment with their reality.

One woman, Nadia, came to our workshop and introduced herself as the executive director of a large non-profit with a master's degree. Through her genogram, we learned that she grew up in Puerto Rico. Her mother had been abused by her father until her mother left him and raised Nadia on her own. When we asked Nadia how her mother was able to leave, she responded: through hard work. Her mother had apparently worked two and sometimes three jobs to save the money to run away from Nadia's father, eventually moving to the United States, where she continued to work very hard for the rest of her life. Nadia told us that she had a son in his early twenties who was pursuing an advanced degree and that she didn't see a lot of him because he was working hard. We asked if she knew what he was passionate about, and Nadia was unable to answer. We asked what messages about work and money she had conveyed to him. Did they discuss his choices? Did he know that she would want him to pursue something he loved? She realized that she had never had that conversation with him, that she was raising her son to focus on working hard, rather than working on what he cared about—as if they were still trying to get safe and escape her abusive father.

Another participant, Kasha, a woman in her late twenties, also experienced the revelation of understanding how past experiences impacted her current decision-making. She told us during her "small money" exercise that she had spent two hours on a gorgeous spring afternoon researching buying a book she was looking for on Amazon. She said that she wanted to buy it secondhand to save money (about $7 in her estimation), so she researched each used book seller's history and reviews. When we asked what the language was in her head as she decided which book to buy, she responded, "I don't want anyone to take advantage of me." As we did Kasha's genogram, we learned that her parents were immigrants from Eastern Europe who had never told her and her siblings what they had had to do to get out of their country of origin and make it to the United States; the story was shrouded in secrecy. Now they ran a very successful business that Kasha and her siblings were raised to work in. She told us that her parents had two employees whose full-time jobs were to review all receipts and make sure that everything was accounted for "down to the penny." When we asked how her parents talked about money, she said, "they told us not to ever let anyone take advantage of us." We asked whether she had considered spending a beautiful spring afternoon doing something other than spending hours researching secondhand books, which she said she had not considered. Kasha then turned to Betsy and asked, "what would you have done?" Betsy replied, "I would have paid the $7 and bought myself two hours." "That never occurred to me," Kasha repeated.

These are just two examples of what happens when a premise is transmitted intergenerationally but not reevaluated in a different context. In both stories, Nadia and Kasha were operating from a premise that worked well for their families in their parents' generation, and kept them safe. Neither, however, considered how that premise might or might not keep them safe in their current situation.

Spotting Patterns, Premises, and Language

When facilitating the mapping of the money-focused genogram, it is helpful to write down the premises, ideas, and language that seem significant as a participant's narrative unfolds. The ability to help our participants recognize patterns in their genograms is a skill we have developed over decades of work. While each professional will develop their own skills and intuitions, this process also merits some guidance regarding how to become aware of patterns in money-focused genograms.

Patterns are best seen visually, with the facilitator constructing the genogram and incorporating the nature of relationships. While drawing the genogram, it is helpful to know ahead of time that patterns or themes (usually in relational dynamics or roles) often exist, which allows the facilitator to be on the lookout for them.

When inquiring about beliefs in one's family of origin, it is helpful to ask participants where these beliefs came from and how they might have been reflected in the family's behavior. Often, these are the access points to unearth a repeated pattern that might have become recurring but lost its original meaning. For instance, if a person who has experienced a shift in class says, "I need a paycheck to feel safe," it would be helpful to understand where that idea is coming from and to follow up with an exploration of their financial reality. How much savings do they have? Have they accumulated a reserve? Do they have investments? An IRA? The responses will give a deeper understanding of whether there is a gap between the feeling of needing a paycheck and the reality. These practices often begin as "inherited behaviors," just as a custom where "we always have the head of the family give a toast or speech before starting our meal" or "we always celebrate Christmas." But in most cases, it is important to ask whether these are "customs" or "traditions," what significance they transmit, and whether they represent the family's reality today.

These behaviors can also arise from social context. We might see certain patterns in immigrant families or families of wealth. Some other potential patterns might originate in an original survival story, a fostered dependency, mystery or secrecy, greed, sexism, or shame.

Another axis worth following is repeated language and meaning in a particular family context. If specific language was used by a grandparent, does it still have the same meaning it might have had when the grandparent used it? How has that language been transmitted? Does it still resonate in someone's head? It is always helpful to explore language and its meaning especially as it might relate to money, work, and class.

When a clinician does a money-focused genogram, we are suggesting that they listen carefully to the language used as well as the patterns that might be recreated. Our practice is to explore and engage with the participant as we collect the information, asking the questions we have recommended. After you have practiced doing a few of these, we can predict that these things will surface.

Graphics of Genogram

Step One: Familial membership and nature of relationships with specific questions about money

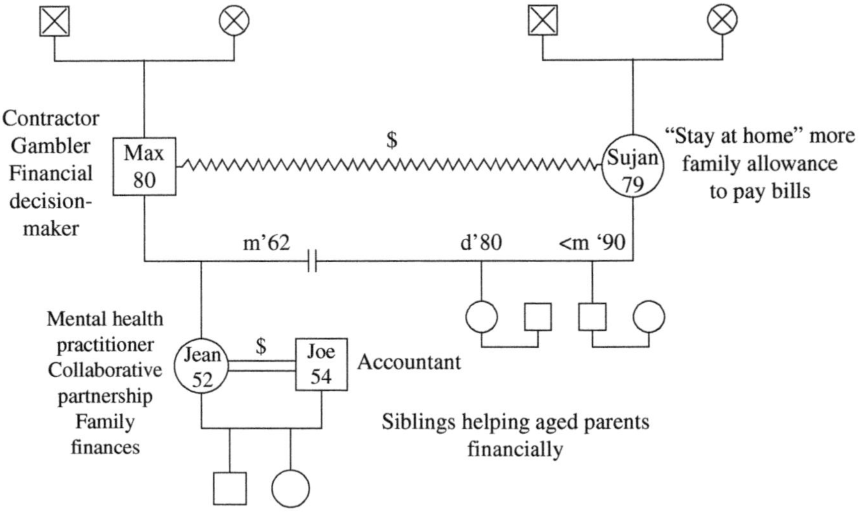

1) Map familial membership and nature of relationships
2) Explore nature of work and familiar meaning of success
3) Explore how money is discussed and attitudes conveyed
4) Ask about parents' management at money during growing-up years

Step Two: Socioeconomic standing: class, cultural, or ethnic background, immigration status/history

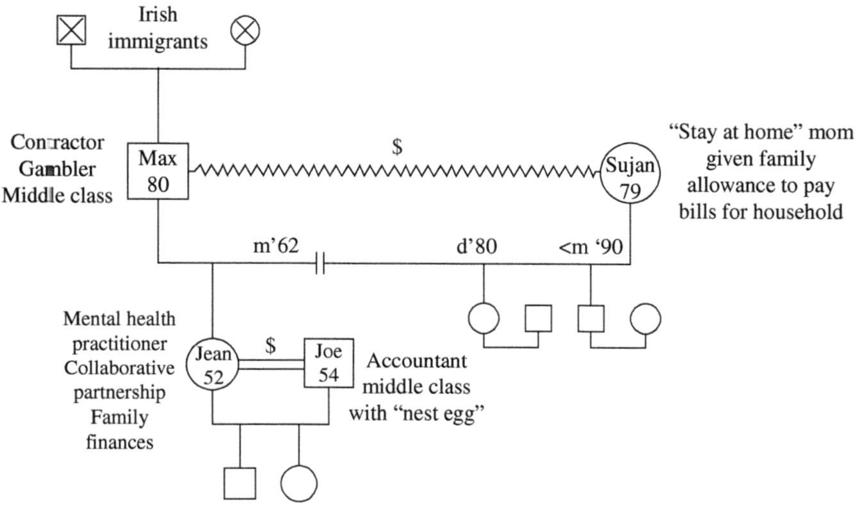

1) What is/was immigration status and how did it shift?
2) What shifts took place in socioeconomic standing; class, culture, racial, or ethnic background?

Step Three: Major Life Cycle Events

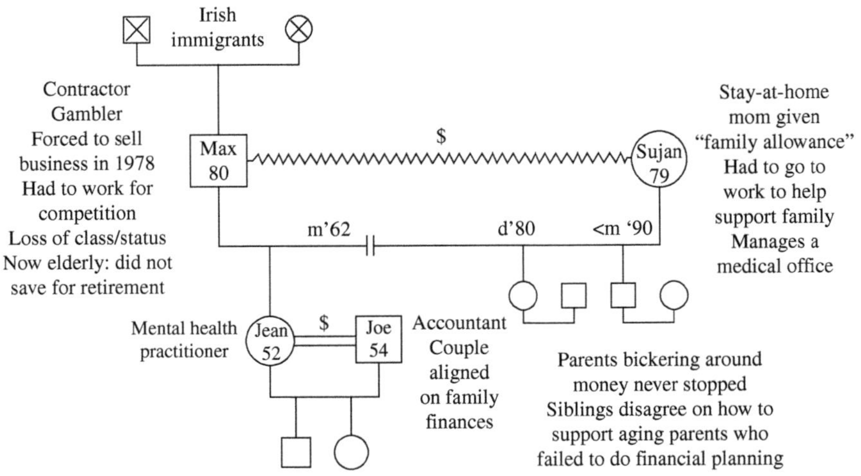

1) If there was a job loss, business sale, big financial deal, how did this affect family?
2) Were there big changes in lifestyle?
3) How old were you when this happened and what's your memory of that titme?
4) If there was a death, divorce, or illness, how did any of these events affect the financial picture for the family?
5) How has the significant event affected you and money in your present life?

Step Four: Recurring Patterns

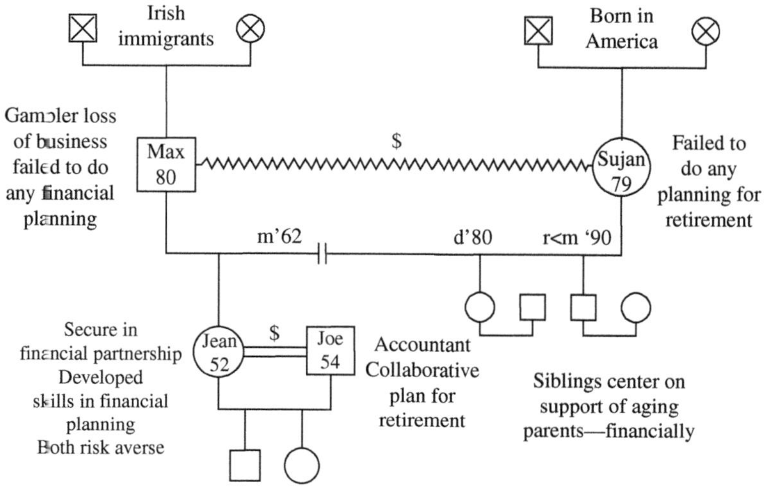

1) Are there "gendered roles" around money? If so, how did they manifest?
2) Does one partner act with strong desire to be taken care of?
3) What is meaning of money in terms of safety and security? How has this been transmitted?

Workshop Sequence for Your Personal Journey

7

We believe that for you our reader to integrate what participants in our workshop have learned, you need to do more than read about what they gleaned; you need to do the work yourself. While we wish that everyone could join us for an in-person workshop experience, we know that is not possible and so we want to offer you, our readers the space to explore these themes on your own. Though you will not have peers around you—pulling you out of isolation, offering you their stories, and listening compassionately to yours–there are also benefits to privacy and quiet. Although, if you want to bring together a group of your own peers and create a self-directed workshop, we support that! In the meantime, take the prompts below and get to work. We hope you will give yourself time to do each exercise and keep your own written notes. More than that, we hope you will return to this part of the book and develop a practice of reflecting on this way of thinking and relating to money in your life and in your clinical practice.

Let's begin the way we begin our workshop: Hi, it's good to meet you! We are glad you are here to explore your money identity. Please try not to judge yourself and instead approach this exploration with curiosity and gentleness.

Exercise One: Hot Start

On a blank piece of paper or below, please respond to these prompts and then complete one or more of the sentences below the questions. Write as much or as little as you want, and when you are finished, you can put it aside.

- What are the first thoughts that come to your mind about money?
- What are the earliest messages you remember about money?
- Do you remember who said them to you?
- Fill in these prompts:
- My mother used to say that ________ (about money).
- My grandfather taught me how to ________ (about money).
- My father always said ________ (about money).

Are there other messages about money that you want to share here? From friends? Siblings? People in your community? Are there voices in your head that you want to write down? Please do!

Exercise Two: Reflection

You bought this book, and you read most of it.

Find a quiet spot if you can. Think back to how you came to reading this book. What motivated you to explore this topic? Did you discuss it with colleagues, friends, or family? Please write down your uncensored thoughts. We want you to revisit your earlier questions, frustrations, and hurdles, as well as your hopes and ambitions. Use this space to write notes to yourself. On the topic of money, where have you found difficulty? Where would you like to find ease? What are you curious about? What fears or reservations do you have?

Exercise Three: Interview

Imagine you are interviewing yourself. Please bring the same compassion and openness you would bring to a new client or a new friend. We would like you to ask yourself the questions in our workshop partner interviews.

Please write down your answers in the space we have provided. Write as full an answer as you can. We suggest you do not edit. Remember this is for you to understand your own relationship to money in a fuller way.

Here are the questions:

- If you have a partner, do you and your partner talk about money, and if so, how often? Do you and your best friend talk about money? With whom do you talk about money?
- If you have children, do you talk to them about money, and if so, in what way? Are there questions they ask that make you uncomfortable?
- Do you talk to your parents/family of origin in the same way about money now as you did when you were a child? Are there limits or prohibitions on talking about money within your family?
- Are there questions about money you want to ask but have not? Why? Is this because you don't know whom to ask or because you have reservations about asking?

Exercise Four: A Small Money Decision

Think of a decision you made to spend a small amount of money (whatever that amount means to you). We are looking for a decision that you deliberated about—should I or shouldn't I spend this money? It should be a decision that you made by yourself, not one you discussed with another person. Please choose a case where you spent an amount of money you would not notice if it were missing from your wallet ($1? $5? $75?)—whatever the number is for you.

Now we are going to ask you to listen to that debate. To do that, we suggest you close your eyes, try to feel the supportive surfaces of your seat, and take some time to actively relax your body and hear your breathing. Then ask yourself: what did the voice say to you that said, "don't spend that money?" What did the other voice that said "go ahead and spend it" say? What specific language did both voices use?

Write down what those voices said. As you are writing, listen for a deeper voice underneath the reflexive language.

Now, let's again quiet our minds and focus on our breathing. Get curious about these voices. Roll them over in your mind. Is there something underneath their words? Is there other language below the surface of the original words? Probe your own answers. For example, if your "don't spend the money" voice said "I can't spend that much"—prompt yourself—"I can't spend that much *because . . .*" or "*because then I . . .*" to see if you can push a little bit past the reflexive and sometimes vague first response into language that is deeper and more specific, personal, and emotional.

We encourage you to take this exercise with you in your day-to-day life. Allow it to bring you some awareness and consciousness in your multiple everyday choices around money.

Exercise Five: Values as a Language

We discovered early on in our research that facilitating conversations within families about money is extremely important and can bring about a deeper understanding of the family system. Importantly, using values as a framework can produce generative family conversations about money. To do this, it is important to first articulate one's core values. This is the first exercise for using values as a language.

Please access the template cards in the appendix. Cut them up so you have each value on its own card, along with the accompanying bullet points.

First Card Sort:

These value cards name both qualities of being and areas of importance. A value is printed on the top of each card. Under each heading, bullet points are meant to stimulate your thinking about the meaning of those values for your own life. This first card sort is to help you articulate your four–five core values. This entails two steps.

1. Separate the cards into two piles (with no set number in either pile), creating a stack of "more important values" and "less important values." You may have difficulty in discriminating between the two, but do your best to create two distinct piles.
2. Now, narrow the more important values to your top four or five. The objective is to identify core values and distinguish between core values and situational values. Core values are those premises that inform a person's behavior whether at work, at home, or with friends. No matter which one of our multiple identities we are inhabiting—be it colleague, spouse, parent, child, friend, or sibling—these values define us. Once you've chosen your core values, please write them below and jot down what your thought process was in choosing them.

Second Card Sort:

Now, reshuffle the cards and think about your most recent serious larger financial decision. Such decisions might be moving to a new neighborhood, changing apartments (bigger? smaller?) financing a home, purchasing a car, planning a vacation, deciding to take or leave a job, deciding to return to school, or developing an annual budget.

Consider the values that informed that decision. Choose the four values from the cards that best describe them. Our first question is: did you discuss the underlying values with anyone? If you decided to move to a larger apartment that is less convenient so that your teenage kids could have their own room, did you explain that to them? If you chose to change jobs in order to have more time with your family did you explain that? If you chose not to buy a car or move to a more expensive neighborhood because that would have required you to leave a job that aligns with your values, or to work an extra job that would pull you away from something else important to you, did you tell your family the underlying reasons? We ask because as we have said repeatedly, we believe leaving gaps in understanding within families is not optimal. It merits examining how explicit we are with our family and loved ones about our choices regarding money as it does send a message about our values.

Our second question is: How do the values that informed your large financial choice compare to the values you chose in the first card sort? Are they the same or different? For many people, there will be contradictions. We believe contradictions are natural and normal. Gaining awareness of the tensions between what we think and say, on the one hand, and what we do, on the other, can help in developing a more thoughtful attitude toward money, a more integrated sense of self, and great compassion for ourselves and others. Our objective in highlighting this tension is twofold: to allow you to accept and integrate your own variability and discrepancies, and to give you a way to talk about them. Making discrepancies explicit and acknowledging their normalcy enhances communication about such topics in most relationships. That enhanced communication leads to greater closeness.

Exercise Six: Vignette

We want to offer you an additional exercise, a series of vignettes. Over the course of our workshops, both with clinicians and non-clinicians, we have found it helpful to work with a variety of vignettes. When we had two full days with non-clinicians, we always included vignettes describing couples and families. Because we had to reduce the workshop to a single day for clinicians who needed to return to their practices, we did not have the time needed to include the vignettes in what has become our standard workshop. That said, we find that vignettes that set up common hurdles and issues are useful to work through.

For this exercise, we are going to give you a case vignette. We'd like you to read it and think about how you might pursue questioning if you were the therapist for this couple. Please write down all the options you can think of. It will be helpful to your understanding of how you consider class, race, and money in a given situation.

> *Denise is a CSW who left her work in a city agency to start a private practice a year ago. She has been seeing two clients, Ellie and Luis, for a few weeks. They tell her that they are 60 years-old and have been*

together since college. Ellie grew up in an economically comfortable family in the suburbs and has enjoyed her career as a dermatologist. Luis grew up in a Dominican-American family and neighborhood and is the first person in his family to go to college. Ellie talks about retiring at 65, traveling the world, keeping their 3-bedroom house, and "enjoying the good things in life."

Five years ago, after a long and unhappy career as a real estate broker, Luis quit to become a musician and composer and feels fulfilled—for "maybe the first time ever." He would like to continue to create and play music and says that he is happy to downsize or move so that they can afford it. They arrive at Denise's office feeling distant from each other and struggling to communicate and feel close.

As you read the vignette and think about the couple's story, what thoughts are surfacing for you? What are the threads you will choose to explore?

Will you ask any financial questions? If so, what are they? If you don't ask financial questions, will you ask about values and priorities?

Dan, a man in his late 20s, comes in to therapy saying he is "in so much debt," that he feels trapped and that he is sure he "will never get out of it." His therapist asks "how much debt?" and he replies "so much, I can't tell my parents, I'm so ashamed."

We encourage therapists to consider a couple of questions: how do you help take the anxiety level down for such a client? And, how do you know how much of what a client in your practice is telling you is purely psychological and how much is based on their actual financial circumstances? We believe the answer to both questions is *the numbers* (which, again we call the data). How would you gather the data in this instance? How could you break down this task into small pieces that could be managed by such a client?

Exercise Seven: Money-Focused Genogram

This exercise will take some time, and you can do it all at once or in pieces. Here are the steps:

1. *Membership*. Start with mapping the members of your family and, using the genogram graphic (reference), include the nature of the relationship.

2. *Class*. For each person, ask: what is or was their socioeconomic standing? What was or is their socio-economic identity? Was it the same as their actual standing? What was their level of education? Did they feel like an "insider" or an "outsider" in society? Did they experience life as full of choices, or did they feel oppressed? Did they have prestige from their job or education or standing in their community? Were they born in this country, or did they emigrate here? Did they consider themselves "middle class," "working class," "poor," or "upper class?" Did that change over time? Did their socioeconomic standing change in either direction over the course of their lives? How did it compare to their parents or children's class standing?
3. *Work*. Then ask: what did they do to make money? Did they have a salaried job? Were they a professional? Did their work make them a lot of money? Did it give them satisfaction? Were they frustrated in their work? Did it feel beneath them? What did they say about work? What did work mean to them over and above providing income for their family? Did it satisfy a family obligation? Did it fulfill their parents' dreams? Did it fulfill an expectation about them as men or women? Did it satisfy them intellectually or artistically or suit their competitiveness? Were they stuck in a job they did not like? And for a parent who did not work, what did they say about not working?
4. *Day-to-Day Handling of Money*. The next step is to consider how money was handled by each person vis-à-vis the other people with whom they were in relationship. So how did your grandmother and your father handle money between them? How did your mother and her siblings? How do you and your partner? You and your children? Do you have clear expectations? Are people honest and up front with each other? Is their favoritism? Is there conflict? Guilt? What does each person in your genogram expect from others?
5. *Language*. Lastly, how do people talk to each other about money? Is there silence? Shaming? Demands? What are the words you recall hearing? What language about money do you associate with each person?
6. *Mysteries or Secrets*. As you move through this exercise, pay attention to what you *do not know* as well as to what you *do know*. Write down what you don't know. Sometimes the mysteries are as informative as the memories. Are there ways for you to get answers to any of the holes in your understanding? Is there someone in your family who might be willing to discuss it with you? Would old photographs or journals help?

7. *Major Life Cycle Events*. Have there been any major life cycle events or crises, such as divorce, illnesses, or deaths, that have occurred in your family that might have had a rippling impact both financially and emotionally? If you were too young at the time, perhaps there is an aunt, parent, grandparent, cousin, uncle, or neighbor who could answer some questions as to how the event affected your family.

   Patterns. Now that you have a visual map and have written down how money and class showed up in your family of origin, it is time to look for patterns, themes, or repeated language or attitudes. While each family is individual and the details of yours will no doubt be very specific, there are some themes we have come across regularly. We think it's worth offering you some prompts to help you find patterns.

- Were people treated differently within your family according to gender? If so, how?
- Were roles regarding money assigned? By whom? What were they?
- Do you see dependency play out across generations?
- How did messages about money change over generations? Are you perpetuating or changing the message you send to your children?
- Does your family genogram show a change in class at any point? Does behavior change at that point? Does attitude?
- Does your family genogram show a change in financial stability at any point? Does that affect behavior or attitude?
- Is the language used by anyone in the family genogram alive today? Do you hear yourself saying what someone in previous generations used to say? Does it seem relevant today in the way it was then?

Use the space below to write down any patterns, themes, or relational dynamics that appear.

More questions to ponder and reflect:

- How did your parents manage money during your childhood?
- Were there any significant messages that were conveyed, implicitly or explicitly?
- How would you describe your parents' beliefs about money? What did they believe money was *for*? Would you say the same was true for your grandparents? Other people in your family?
- Do you manage money similarly or differently from what you saw growing up?

- Have you and your siblings ever talked about money management in your family?
- What emotions come up for you around money: fear or guilt; pride or shame; greed or envy; power or powerlessness?
- Do you think your mother or father feels or felt these same emotions?
- Are there differences between you and your family of origin in handling and talking about money?
- Are there any themes or patterns that emerge for you as we do this?

Some of these questions might resonate while others may not. Please take the time to look at your genogram and ask yourself which questions might be relevant to your life experience around money, work, or class.

Please note that one can put a genogram away and come back to it weeks, months, or even years later and see or add information at any point. The genogram is merely a tool that allows us to see graphically what we might not have been conscious of. Use it as it suits your journey of pursuing your relationship to agency around money.

Section Three

Application and Case Reviews

Follow the Money Application

8

There have been consistent requests in our Workshops from mental health practitioner participants asking us for "more"—more practice addressing money in their own lives, more facilitated discussion with their peers as they try to overcome their own inhibitions and conflicts around money, and more guidance on integrating money in their work with clients.

As we have said earlier in the book, we are not inventing or promoting a new kind of therapy. We are offering a new tool to use for exploration and assessment. That tool is money. We believe money is a means of expanding our awareness of ourselves and others. It is a tool that can expand and enrich your practice.

However, integrating and applying what we have taught will be made harder by the social prohibitions against talking about money, prohibitions that intrude on therapists as much they do on clients. It is a subject fraught with emotional charge and connections. Integrating this new perspective for yourself and applying it in your work will take time and practice.

Developing awareness of your own multigenerational patterns around money will likely bring your awareness to the thread of money in your client's lives. Being curious about your relational patterns around money and the narratives in your head will also have the effect of curiosity about the same with your clients'.

Because this issue is not addressed and practiced in most academic/supervisory settings, we have considered how this book can fill the gap to support your evolving skills. This Chapter will support your capacity to "follow the money" by speaking directly and neutrally about money and recognizing relational patterns around money. There are discreet competencies: working against the prohibition on discussing money—in fact announcing that your client is safe to talk about it, moving to normalize talking about money, collecting data on how money is handled in a client's, or couple's lives and spotting financially based relational patterns. We give you a sense at the end of the chapter of where you will end up—doing what we refer to as "practical and emotional toggling," moving back and forth fluidly between the practical (money) and the emotional effortlessly as you attempt to neutralize the connection. Throughout you are paying attention to yourself, to your own reluctance to talk about money, to your reaction to the financial information you are hearing to help you develop the objectivity needed to do this work.

Like Every Other Skill: Examining Your Inquiry

A critical skill for all mental health practitioners is considering their line of inquiry. For our purposes, the choice and challenge often are the timing around when to follow the money pattern and when to pursue the emotional issue. It requires that you, as the clinician, observe and think about where each question you ask takes the process. Which choice point might lead to greater understanding? Are you comfortable with financial language? Do you have command of the basic terms? In addition, how do you push through societal and personal tendencies to avoid talking about money? How do you help your clients push through their avoidance?

Neutralize the Charge and Normalize the Conversation

The first step for a therapist is to make the transition from the rules around money "outside the therapist room" to rules around money "inside the therapist room." Announcing that money is going to be discussed indicates that it is safe to do so, that you are not afraid of it, that within this context you and your clients will not be abiding by the social and familial prohibitions, and that it is important and central, just like all the other parts of your collaborative exploration with them. You may choose to say, "while outside this room I know it is very difficult to discuss this but here we are going to treat it like every other facet of your life," or you may simply inquire with a neutral stance. Those initial moments will matter. You may want to consider how you approach it.

Secondly, can you easily ask questions about financial data, that is, cash flow, net worth, budget, investment portfolio, and so on? Are these words familiar or foreign to you? Are you familiar with the financial data in your own family life? If you were in the client's seat and were asked these sorts of questions, how would you respond? Your comfort level with the financial conversation will affect the client's comfort to respond.

Exercise for Financial Language

As an exercise for yourself, please review your own family financial information. What are all the inflows—both where do they come from and how much are they? Are they consistent or sporadic? What are the outflows; where does your family spend its money exactly? Do you have all the information you need to find out the full answers? Do you know all sources of income? all sources of expenses? If not who else holds that information? Can you create a list of your family assets, i.e. house, car, investment portfolio, retirement funds, art, anything else that has monetary value? Is this information easily accessible to you? If not, what stands in the way of accessing it? How would you characterize your financial dynamic with any other adults in your house? In relational dynamics, there is often an unspoken agreement around money. Can you describe your unspoken agreements?

Take a moment to reflect on what you have written down and whether there is a gap between what you determined is real and what you thought might have been. For example, did you have a story in your head before beginning that "we are in so much debt" only to find out that while you're in debt, it is manageable given your income? Do you have a mortgage, a line of credit? Did you think "my partner handles everything I don't know where it all is or how much there is" only to find out that over time you now know all the facts? Did you think "my partner has told me I spend too much" and now you see that your partner outspends you or is on par with your spending? If there is a gap, can you figure out the "why"? Are you having a reaction to doing this exercise? Take the time to process for yourself what your experience has been and observe whether something changes for you in the clinical space? Are you any more open to the discussion around money with your clients.

Find the Relational Dynamic

Isaiah and Kamisha are an African-American couple, and had been married for 20 years. They both work: she as a therapist and he in the technology industry. They live in New York City. They have 2 children, a son who is launched and living on his own and a younger daughter who is entering her last year of college.

Kamisha started by stating her concern about how much money they had spent this past summer on a family vacation. She made sure to share what a wonderful time they had and how great it was for everyone. Her worry was more about their financial circumstances. Isaiah said perhaps they had spent more than they should have, but he felt it was worth it, and it would all work out. Kamisha then articulated more of her worries, citing other areas where she anticipated bills that would be due, such as tuition, insurance, and taxes. One could hear the anxiety in her voice. Isaiah appeared irritated and said, "It will all work out"!

Questions:

When you hear this vignette:

1. What are you listening for?
2. What are you observing?
3. How do they listen to each other?
4. How do they respond?
5. As their process unfolds, what are your initial thoughts and what questions do you ask to explore the beginning of a working hypothesis?

In listening to their story unfold, we want to encourage you to listen closely to the problem as the couple presents it. Observing the interactive dynamic between the couple provides a good beginning.

Choice/Decision

The choice we see here is between identifying and characterizing the money relational dynamic versus inquiring if the couple relates to each other in this way more broadly. For example, we might ask "Kamisha, do you find Isaiah protective of you in other areas of your life together? Does he consistently reassure you about your worries about all things or just about money?" If indeed she confirms that it is only around money, it informs our next step which is to explore more deeply with them their understanding of why this dynamic around money is different and how each of them understands that difference. If she/he confirms that this pattern is generally reflective of their dynamic, then as therapist you might shift your line of inquiry.

The goal here is to see if you, the clinician and your clients have gathered enough information to establish if this is a dynamic exclusively around money or a more consistent relational pattern.

Choice

This juncture presents the choice between pursuing the emotional mining for the interpersonal dynamic and/or specifically the money dynamic. Before jumping to any conclusions, more exploration is required—a deeper understanding of what the "real" difference in perspective is about. So, perhaps a deeper exploration of each perspective might be advisable.

Here are questions you might be thinking about:

1. How would you acknowledge/query the different perspectives?
2. Would you wonder, state, or query about the interactive pattern you are observing around money?
3. Would you choose "labels" like worrier/ protector/soother?

The choice point here would be to understand more specifically if this relational pattern is specific to their money management together.

Question: As you progress in this initial interview, would you be attempting to develop an operational hypothesis? Is that hypothesis flexible enough for change as new information surfaces? And key to understanding this evolving thought process? How might you check it out? An initial operative dynamic might be described as "Kamisha worries, and Isaiah tries to dispel her worries and move on." Does this hypothesis give you an idea of how this couple interacts? If you are considering this as a repeated pattern between them, what might be a way to examine this? This is when you might begin to formulate an intervention to either confirm or dispel your operational hypothesis. This is where you might explore if this pattern occurs repeatedly around worries about everything or just when money is the topic. As a next step in your hypothesis development, you might use the "money issue" to amplify your initial hypothesis. The best way to do this would be asking directly about their financial circumstances to understand what is real and what is a dynamic.

As an intervention, you might begin to question how they manage their finances. Do they share finances, do they share their financial information, or do they keep their financial lives separate? Do they split their costs, share them based on their incomes, or do something else? Do they have an agreed upon method or is it ad hoc? Is it explicit or implicit? Do they do any budgeting? If so, how often do they review the budget together? Have they sat down to look at the financial picture? Perhaps this is something they could do before the next meeting as it would be helpful to understand together what the financial problem might be.

This intervention is a very practical one, but the result will quickly lead you to identify whether there is a broader dynamic of Kamisha worrying and Isaiah "downplaying" the worry, rather than his acknowledging, empathizing, and then addressing the financial issue collaboratively with Kamisha. This might be where the therapy work begins.

What we learn from this vignette is multifaceted. We see that "how money is dealt with" can often reveal a relational dynamic. To explore more, we ask the couple to put together financial information to have a clearer picture for themselves.

There is a difference between asking specific financial questions and/or asking the couple to sit down together to prepare the information. What we're thinking through intuitively is: would the couple be so uncomfortable doing the work in the session that it would be a waste of time, or do we think they might be able to do this on their own and it's worthwhile trying? Do we think more about their relational dynamic will come out if we attempt to do the work in session or out of session. These are all questions for which there is no "right answer." For a practitioner, this is a matter of learning over time and developing instincts. Whether they do this or not, more information for the hypothesis development will surface. And then, if they can do it, we do not know what they will discover. We are asking them to prepare the information for themselves and when they return, we will ask them what they have discovered and explore that with curiosity. We will also ask how it went? If they are unable to do it, we will inquire about what got in the way and incorporate that into our work with the couple.

Our stance is to collaborate with them—to find the practical information that we hope will lead us to the emotional dynamic and explore what might block them from accessing the financial information.

Follow the Money: Find Out What's Real

Mary and Louise came in holding hands. They shared that they had just celebrated their third-year anniversary. After acknowledging their celebration, I asked what brought them in today. Louise stated that everything in their relationship was perfect except their finances. Mary was continuously reprimanding Louise for overspending and Louise would counter with claiming that Mary was "cheap," a miser. This was the only area in their life that caused them tension. They wanted help with it.

It is critically important for the therapist and client to establish the financial reality of their circumstances. By this, we mean getting all the financial data. In this vignette, the couple is articulating quite clearly their understanding of the discrepancy. As a result, it is important to explore with the couple their financial situation to understand what this discrepancy is about. How much income do they each have? How have they set up their finances? Do they have a joint account? Do they each keep separate accounts in addition? Have they developed a working budget for themselves? This allows everyone working together with the same information to clearly see the reality of their money situation and how that compares to the story each carry about themselves and each other.

In this specific situation, it appears that asking financial questions would be in alignment with the presenting problem. Here is a specific case where, without the actual numbers we would be unable to clarify which is story and which is real?

In this case, what we discovered was that Louise actually had additional funds that she was receiving from a trust fund that had been set up by her grandmother. For some reason, she had never disclosed that information to Mary. She became quite apologetic and said it had been a complete oversight. Her "overspending" was with funds she was getting from that source. She contributed from her salary, as did Mary for their joint account. Their common budget did not include the monies she received from the trust. Because it had been so separate, she never thought to discuss it with Mary. They walked out of the office arm in arm feeling quite content.

When a client or couple comes into the office presenting a money problem, it is usually easier to collect the financial information earlier in the engagement. In other situations where it is not clear whether pursuing the money theme will help to reveal more information, the therapist has to intuit whether or not getting the financial information will be useful and why. Sharing that with the clients will probably make the exchange smoother.

Now that we have both dynamics and data—how and when do we toggle?

Clara came in very anxious about living in retirement and on her own. She had been very successful in her career and been recognized for her competence. She had recently retired and lost her husband of 40 years.

We began by talking about her marriage, which she described as wonderful, and moved into talking about her work mostly in non-profit management. Initially we discussed her mourning her husband as well as the loss of her job. We explored some of her ideas about what to do with her time. None of this seemed to be the cause of her anxiety, but it would have been inappropriate to skip over the new and deeply emotional losses of her husband and her lifelong career.

Clara reported that she routinely called the woman who managed her investments to ask for funds and would anxiously ask "is it ok? Will I be alright?" That seemed like it might be fertile ground to explore since it seemed at odds with the competence she displayed in her work. We discussed her financial circumstances. It turned out that she was living from a pension and social security and her investments. We discussed her budget and her investments which were significant. Neither of us saw a reason objectively to doubt that she was not overspending given her savings. Next, we explored in more depth how she handled money with her money manager. How often did she ask for funds? Was it by email or by phone? What exactly was the conversation? Clara was calling sometimes weekly to request funds, and each time she was asking for reassurance. Her manager routinely told her that she was "ok" and "living comfortably within her means," but her anxiety persisted.

It felt like time to move out of the question of the practical. A line of inquiry around gender and emotions did not yield any insight into her anxiety. She and her husband shared finances and decision-making. Next, we discussed Clara's family upbringing. Her family was working class, second generation immigrants from South America. They had all had successful long-term careers in government and union jobs. She had witnessed her family enjoying the security of those careers, and her parents had taught her that getting a paycheck ensured economic security, and thereby, safety.

This lesson, taught based on her class identity felt critically important. We discussed the psychology of her class jump from the security of a union or government paycheck to living off pension/social security and if needed, investments. We use the term "class jump" to mean a shift in financial circumstances that brings along with it a shift in class status, though not perhaps in class identity. In Clara's family, money was completely transactional. It was used to pay for "food, clothing and shelter." It was also a source of safety so long as it was being earned in a regular salary. In Clara's new reality, besides her income from her pension and social security, her investments were giving off dividends and interest. Her money was making money for her. This was a completely new concept for Clara to appreciate and integrate.

Ultimately, we returned to the practical and discussed what it would feel like if rather than asking her investment manager to "give" her money when she "needed it"—she instead put together an annual budget, divided by twenty-six, and asked for a "distribution" to be sent every two weeks, just like a paycheck. Clara said, "well, that would feel great."

It was by toggling back and forth from her initial anxiety to her finances, to her nuclear family to her family of origin, and then back to her finances that we arrived at the premise that was informing her anxiety. When we made this connection, she understood immediately that she was operating from a multi-generational inherited belief that equated safety with a regular paycheck. She was living within an identity that did not apply to her financial picture in the present. We came up with the above plan based on a deeper understanding of her identity and her needs and the reality she was living in.

In our work, we have come to appreciate how class plays an important role in money identity. The perspective that different class cultures apply to money and what a paycheck means is just one example of this. It is for that reason that we believe it is important to pay attention when you see a shift in class from one generation to the next. The transition of a person or a family from more or less fiancial security and to more or less social status is not automatically accompanied by a comprehensive integration of that change. Clara had worked hard throughout her professional life and had accumulated a nice nest egg. She could not embrace that as financial security, and this manifested in two ways: her anxiety around retirement and "how would she pay her bills?" and her need to keep a large amount of cash in her bank account against her financial adviser's judgment.

Moving from financial "fact" to emotional reactivity is what we mean by toggling.

Here is another case example of how toggling can be effective. The challenge for the therapist is to seamlessly move from the emotional to the practical.

> *John, a 35-year-old man, described the escalation of his anxiety around the time that he and his wife learned that she was pregnant with twins. They had a 3-year-old daughter, and this news propelled him into the high anxiety he described. He connected his anxiety to the overwhelming responsibility he was feeling as the "head" of the family. After exploring what those symptoms were, and recognizing that these were manageable, we moved into a picture of his economic circumstances. He had been a self-employed commercial photographer for the past decade. Pre-pandemic, he had been doing very well financially. And now he was describing his business as "slow." To get a clearer financial picture, we looked at his income pre-pandemic and his income now. He had experienced a 50% drop in income. We acknowledged that some of his anxiety was connected to this reality. We talked about his work options moving forward. We looked at short term and long-term plans. We had him begin to figure out where and how he might be able to bring in more funds. He liked doing "assignments" and gathering information. He was very good with numbers. At one point, I asked how much he shared with his wife, as it seemed to me, he was not bringing her into the "problem solving" process. We moved back and forth from the practical to the emotional. He came back and said he and his wife had had a good conversation, and she was going to begin to work part-time.*

This certainly helped to take the strain off John, and he did what he could to bring in more “business” for himself. Over the 7–8 months that we worked together, we were constantly moving from the emotional to the practical, recognizing his anxiety and connecting it to what might be real and disconnecting it from what he might be imposing. John came from a traditionally conservative family where he believed that he carried the role of provider. This process served John in many ways. He was able to get a different perspective on how he might share the financial responsibility with his wife. He understood that he needed to build back his “book of business” after the pandemic. He also looked for other ways to bring in income. He discovered that he liked working with numbers and could easily help other small businesses.

As a therapist, if you can develop comfort around financial issues, you should be able to then use that in the clinical space. It will help you to uncover information that would take longer to access, including relational dynamics and the emotional meaning of operating premises. It will certainly take time to integrate and apply these ideas.

Introduction to Family Life Cycle

9

In these last two chapters of our book, we will present treatment reviews of nine cases to demonstrate our approach. We will use the family life cycle as our reference point, focusing on transitions that take place as families move from one stage to the next. We use this as a foundational frame because all too often financial issues are present as these transitions take place. We think this is a good format to illustrate our approach.

The family life cycle is a useful conceptual frame for understanding how families evolve over time, navigating key developmental stages with defined tasks. The underlying process of the family life cycle is the negotiation of the expansion, contraction, and realignment of the relationship system to support the entry, exit and development of family members in a functional way.[1] These stages include events like launching, marriage, the birth of children, aging, illness, divorce, remarriage and death, all of which result in both natural transitions as well as transitions with more complicating factors. With movement from one stage to the next, the dynamics of relationships shift, new challenges emerge, and new possibilities open, all while the individual life cycle takes shape as it evolves within the matrix of the family life cycle.

These movements from one stage to another call for an emotional process of transition as well as second-order changes in family status. The transition completes as these emotional tasks are integrated. This defines the completed change. There are specific tasks that require addressing as the family moves through these distinct stages. For instance, as young adults get launched, their differentiation from the nuclear family is a key task. This requires both the young adult becoming more independent as well as the parents' "letting go." There are a multitude of exits and entries into the family system that both parents and young adults must manage and at the same time establish a work/personal life. This is described more fully at the end of this chapter where we have included in both paragraph and chart form the specific tasks for completing these transitions.

Key to these transitions becomes the role shifts in relationships. For instance, in the launching transition (which takes place over a long period of time) the parenting role shifts as the young adult becomes more independent. Please note that some of these are never completed and yet the family moves on. Use this information as a reference point rather than a "fait a complete." As a therapist, it helps you in your understanding of the specific family system and where the family might have detoured in their process.

During treatment, these transitions of the family life cycle present opportunities to open the family system for deeper exploration. This exploration process of the family system affords the clinician the chance to address the family finances.

Money, though a significant factor, is often a taboo subject at these junctures. Yet, ironically, money can be a very important issue to address and provide significant dynamic information about family patterns. We all know that finances can shape major life decisions, influence power dynamics, and contribute to family stress. As we continue to advocate, addressing these hidden financial issues is essential and can reveal these dynamics. This leads to achieving a holistic understanding of the family's emotional and relational systems—helping to ground any new family dynamic in their reality.

For example, the birth of a child may trigger financial anxieties about providing for the family, while anticipating retirement can raise concerns about

1 Carter, Betty and McGoldrick, Monica, eds. The Expanded Family Life Cycle: Individual, Family and Social Perspectives. Boston: Allyn and Bacon, 1999.

long-term financial security. Disruptive events, such as divorce or loss of a job, may also force families to confront their financial stability. The treatment cases we have chosen will reflect how accessible the money issue becomes during these transitions. In these moments, when money is explored, it becomes clear how financial matters intertwine with emotional and relational concerns. Often, however, the topic remains taboo, either because of cultural norms or the discomfort it can provoke in the clinical space for the family, the clinician or both.

The cases we have chosen represent significant transitions in the family life cycle, showcasing how money plays a central yet often unspoken role in family dynamics. We will give an overview of the treatment and show, when money is addressed, both the emotional and practical dimensions of the system shift. Whether it's the struggle to fund a child's education, negotiations over inheritance, or the financial strain of caregiving for elderly parents, money is frequently present but seldom discussed openly. In some cases, families can address these issues head-on, leading to healthier, more transparent relationships. In others, avoidance of financial discussions only perpetuates existing tensions.

The following are the life cycle transitions with the inherent emotional tasks that families and individuals within them navigate during the transition. For a frame of reference while you read the treatment reviews, we are defining each transition and those tasks in a discrete paragraph. You can reference back to these as you read through the case reviews. You can also note how money can become relevant in this process. We have also included a chart as an alternative resource.

Key Transitions in the Family Life Cycle

1. Launching Children

As children transition into adulthood, the family moves from having adolescents to young adults. This launching of children involves a gradual separation process as young adults begin to leave the family home and establish their independence.

This phase can span 10 to 20 years, affecting multiple generations within the family. In the first phase, typically between the ages of 21 and 26, young adults experiment with independence, exploring career paths and personal relationships. The second phase, from 26 to 33, sees them laying the groundwork for more permanent commitments in both work and relationships. Financial considerations play a key role during this period, as families prepare children for financial independence while parents navigate the challenges of transferring financial responsibility. The balance between offering support and fostering autonomy becomes central, as the family transitions through these pivotal life stages.This stage includes multiple generations and is one of the most complex within the family life cycle.

2. The New Couple: Marriage

In the context of marriage, emotional tasks are centered around developing a strong, balanced partnership while navigating both individual and shared growth. One key task is the ability to merge two distinct family systems, which involves negotiating differences in values, traditions, and expectations. Couples must learn to communicate effectively, resolve conflicts, and build a foundation of trust and mutual respect. Emotional differentiation is crucial, allowing each partner to maintain their individual identity while committing to the relationship. Additionally, the couple must establish financial and emotional interdependence, agreeing on roles and responsibilities, especially when navigating significant transitions such as the birth of children or career changes. These emotional tasks foster intimacy, stability, and the capacity to face future challenges together.

3. Starting a Family: Expanding the Family System

Starting a family, whether through birth, adoption, or IVF, impacts the entire family network, reshaping relationships and roles. The arrival of a child solidifies the couple's connection to their extended family, as grandparents, aunts, uncles, and others become more intricately involved in their lives. Couples must navigate the balance between maintaining ties with their larger family while preserving the integrity and boundaries of their nuclear family unit. This stage also introduces shifts in work, lifestyle, and childcare responsibilities, making financial planning essential to meet the demands of raising children while ensuring long-term stability.

4. Later Life

With extended life expectancy, families often encounter a range of new challenges that test their emotional resilience and adaptability. Aging can bring unresolved emotional issues to the forefront, particularly in the context of caregiving and shifting sibling dynamics. The lack of well-established cultural patterns for integrating older generations into the daily rhythms of family life further complicates this period, leaving many families to navigate these transitions without clear guidance. Prominent stressors such as decision-making around caregiving responsibilities, emotional resolutions between parents and their adult children, and balancing the needs of siblings as roles shift can strain relationships. These challenges require intentional effort to foster understanding and manage the emotional complexities that arise in this stage of life. This life stage is characterized by increased stress on the family system, often compounded by financial matters.

5. Major Complications in the Family Life Cycle

Interruptions in the family life cycle, such as illness, death, divorce, remarriage, and loss of job, introduce significant stress that complicates the family's ability to progress through natural transitions. These major crises demand additional emotional and logistical tasks, often delaying key developmental stages for several years. Financial strain frequently compounds these challenges, as unexpected expenses or changes in economic stability add further burdens to the family system. The need to manage both emotional upheaval and financial disruption makes it even more difficult for families to navigate the life cycle's expected transitions smoothly, as these add another layer of complexity to family functioning.

Roadmap

As you read through the case treatment reviews in the next section, please notice three important elements. First and foremost, what is the life cycle stage for the family? Is there a disruption of any sort? What factors complicate this transition? How does talking about money happen, and with what results? And finally, were you able to see how exercises you might have experienced or read about were used? These exercises might serve as catalysts for shifting treatment. When an exercise is mentioned in the case review, it would serve you to go back to the chapter describing the exercise to review and understand how it is being used.

This structure effectively frames the case studies to focus on the family's life cycle stages, complications, and how discussing money influences family dynamics.

Key Stages and Tasks of Family Life Cycle

This framework provides a detailed look at key stages in the family life cycle, emphasizing the inherent emotional and financial tasks that families must navigate. Here is a summary of the transitions and tasks:

1. Couplehood/Marriage:
   - The marriage involves two entire systems merging to create a third.
   - Couples navigate issues of money, sex, time, power, friends, in-laws, and daily tasks.
   - Major goal: form a marital system and realign relationships with extended family and friends to include one's spouse.
   - Challenges: negotiating differences (financial, educational, etc.) and multigenerational patterns.
2. Starting a Family:
   - Having children affects the entire family network, regardless of how the child is born or adopted.
   - Childbirth solidifies the couple's connection to the extended family.
   - Couples balance connecting with the larger family while maintaining the integrity of the nuclear family.
   - Shifts in work and childcare require financial planning.
3. Launching Children:
   - Separation process, with young adults leaving the family home.
   - This phase can last 10–20 years and involves multiple generations.
   - First phase (ages 21–26): young adults experiment with independence.
   - Second phase (ages 26–33): young adults establish a foundation for work and relationships.
   - Considerations around money: preparing children for financial independence and parents' readiness to transfer financial responsibility.
4. Second Phase of Launching (Partnering and Living Together):
   - Tasks include establishing direction in work, intimate relationships, and maintaining individuality in relation to the family of origin.
   - Key challenges involve addressing money issues, gender roles, fairness, and transparency in relationships.

5. Later Life:
   - Aging introduces new challenges for the family, such as caregiving, unresolved emotional issues, and shifting sibling dynamics.
   - There are few established cultural patterns for incorporating older generations into family life.
   - Prominent stressors include decision-making, caregiving, and emotional resolutions between generations.

Case Reviews

Family Life Cycle Transitions

10

10.1 Ahmet

Initial Contact

I received an email from Ahmet asking if I would have time to see him. He had gotten my contact from his mother, who is a therapist. I responded and suggested some options for us to have a phone conversation. Ahmet introduced himself as a male of Turkish descent. He said he had been quite anxious lately and his mother had suggested he call me. She knew of me from the work I had done at Ackerman.

Ahmet went on to share his story. He and his wife had lived in NYC since they married five years ago. During the pandemic, they decided to move out of the city and bought a condo in New Jersey, which is where they were living. Three months ago, his wife Derya finally got pregnant. They had been trying for a long time. The IVF had finally worked. He felt as though they were out of the precarious time and was finally able to focus on the future. Their last visit to the doctor brought the news that Derya was pregnant with twins. Ahmet said that this news sent him into a tailspin very unexpectedly. He didn't know what happened. He desperately wanted to figure this out! He felt overwhelmed at the thought of his family growing exponentially and his having to support them. His anxiety had become intolerable.

Presenting Problem

Ahmet talked about his constant challenge of trying to manage his anxiety. He had never felt this badly before. Throughout his life, he had been able to neutralize this feeling by talking it through with his mom, sister, or now Derya. It wasn't working and he felt at a loss for what to do. I asked Ahmet if he was able to pinpoint when this had started. He pointed to the day that they discovered they were having two babies not one! Ahmet referred to that moment as the triggering point. Everything from then had gone "downhill." For over a year they had been going through IVF process. It had been torture. I started by asking him what he thought was behind this anxiety, that is, when he heard the news about the babies, what were his first thoughts? Ahmet was able to say that the idea of being responsible for two more human beings felt overwhelming to him. I challenged him by suggesting that he did have a partner, Derya. He came back at me by noting that as the man in the household, he felt overly responsible as provider and protector. By this time, we were coming to the end of our session. I made a mental note to begin next time with exploring Ahmet's work life to get a fuller understanding.

Family Members

In our first session together, Ahmet described his family to me. His parents had been divorced when he was seven years old. Both had remarried, and until his father died a few years ago, he had had good relationships with everyone. Ahmet had a younger sister but no step or half siblings. Neither parent had had any children with their new spouse.

Ahmet began to tell me the story around his father's death and how his stepmother had assumed control of the inheritance that he and his sister thought they were entitled to. Sue, his stepmother, had gotten his father to sign a new will toward the end of his dad's life. Ahmet had been there to take care of his dad but did not realize what was happening. His sister was furious and had stopped talking to Sue. Ahmet had tried to maintain a connection but the more he thought about it the angrier he became. He went on to describe his relationship to his stepdad as being good. As a matter of fact, he depended on him for lots of business advice.

His wife Derya was an only child. Her parents lived in New Jersey and were still both working. They had recently sold their condo and were going to be living with his in laws until they were able to find a house. With two babies coming, they had decided to look for a small house near Derya's parents.

System Context

As described in the introduction of this section, starting a family means introducing new members which then shifts relationships and roles. For instance, Derya and Ahmet would now be husband and wife as well as parents together. Welcoming two babies into their family system would mean sharing responsibility for caring for their newborns as well as shifts in work schedule. In addition there would be financial demands both immediate and long-term. Their relationships to their extended family members would shift as they became responsible for the next generation. The challenge of balancing their couple relationship along with their new parenting roles would bring new challenges. Although Ahmet could not articulate any of the above, he intuitively was understanding the change that was about to take place in their lives.

I wondered which part of this change presented the biggest challenge for him. I started by asking Ahmet if he understood what about the news of twins made him so anxious. He responded by telling me that he felt overwhelmed by the responsibility of being the provider for so many people. Given his age and the knowledge that Derya had worked, I was somewhat surprised to hear his very gendered response. I wondered what that was about. I asked him where that notion of "male provider" came from for him. He referenced his Turkish culture. In that same session, I discovered that Ahmet had been self-employed as a photographer. During the pandemic, there had been very little work and since the pandemic, he felt paralyzed in terms of what to do. I then tracked his work trajectory from first job to present. Ahmet realized early on in his career that he wanted to work in his own business. He had the experience of working in a company and he bridled at the bureaucracy he had experienced. He decided to start his own business five years pre pandemic. He had become adept at the business side of building his business. He described to me how he had proceeded to market himself, the tools he had used. He was also skilled administratively and learned how to set up his books, write his contracts as well as do the creative work efficiently. He had built a successful small business until the pandemic hit. He mentioned his gross net number and calculated his profit for me. I was actually happy to hear him do that as I realized he could manage numbers. It was when I asked him what that number was today, he became silent. It took a few moments for him to compose himself and respond. He shared that it had dropped to half of what it had been. I then understood the crisis he was feeling. I also referenced back to the inheritance issue and reframed it as his "safety net" which he discovered had been taken from him. He agreed.

Treatment

In thinking about Ahmet's situation, I realized part of his burden/anxiety might have been his role in his present family. When he and Derya had married, he had taken full responsibility for their financial life. Because they both were working, there was plenty of income and they were able to save for their future home. They enjoyed a great quality of life in NYC. During the pandemic, they decided to leave the city and buy a condo as their "starter" apartment. I asked how much Derya was involved in their decision-making. He said they made these together. I then asked if she understood how all this effected their finances. He said she shied away from that part. I then asked if she understood how much his business income had dropped. I wondered if he ever talked to Derya about what was happening. He said he talked to her about his emotional state, but they didn't talk about the numbers. I suggested that it would probably be helpful to him if he could tell her what he was struggling with in his business. He said he would do it.

A few weeks later, Ahmet let me know that he had spoken to Derya. She was surprised by the information. They had a long talk about it. She shared with him her initial intention to go back to work after the birth but had been caught off guard herself when they discovered they were having twins. I realized that this would not solve the problem but wondered why she had kept that information to herself. Ahmet went on to say that the conversation had been a very good one for him. He felt relieved and not so alone in his concern about their future. What mattered to him was that she had been thinking about going back to work at some point. This resonated with him and began to dissipate the premise he held of being the "provider, a social gendered role" held by many men and often supported by their partner.

Ahmet still appropriately felt anxious about his business and its potential failure.

We started looking at what his options might be. Should he be looking at doing something different or actually trying to build back his business. I suggested he make a list of options for himself as a next step.

Outcome

Ahmet and I spent the next phase of our work with him working on the options he had come up with. As he began to delve into the choices, we would talk not only about the factual part but his reaction to "going down a new path." He remarked often how helpful this was for him to have an "action plan." He commented how he was identifying new skills that he had never acknowledged. This came about when his friends asked him to help them organize their small business. He was able to put their books in order, help them with their website, and set up their financials. He began to realize that he could help other small businesspeople in the same way. By that time though, some of his steps toward rebuilding his own business began to pan out. What he said did matter to him was the knowledge that he had those newfound skills.

Within a few months of our starting to work together, the new babies were born. Ahmet had to take time off to help with newborns. He said he would return when life calmed down. He also noted how helpful our work had been. He reiterated that when he first reached out to me, he had felt helpless. Although he did not quite feel "out of the woods," that feeling had gone away. He also felt more partnered with Derya and ready to enter this next phase of their family life cycle together in a partnership that he had never thought would be possible. Not only was she his emotional partner, but they were now very definitely "family business" partners. This was most comforting to him.

10.2 Sofia and Bogdan

Initial Contact

Sofia reached out via email to inquire about couples therapy for herself and her husband, Bogdan. A professional colleague had referred her to me. She explained that Bogdan was about to inherit a substantial sum of money from his parents through a trust. While their previous therapy had been beneficial, they felt the need for someone like me to help them navigate this significant transition in their financial situation. Their primary concern revolved around how money affected their dynamic.

Family Membership

In our first session, Sofia shared details about their family. She and Bogdan, both White and Ukranian-American, had been together for twelve years and married for ten. They have three children, aged nine, eight, and five, and reside in Riverdale, where the kids attend public school. Both parents work: Bogdan from home, and Sofia, a physical therapist has an office nearby.

Sofia described her family of origin, mentioning her father's role as a pastor, which necessitated frequent moves. She is the eldest of three siblings, with a younger brother and sister. In contrast, Bogdan, an only child, grew up in Long Island. His parents still live in their family home, and he experienced a family trauma with the loss of a sibling shortly after birth. Bogdan's father had a successful career as a financial consultant and later as a CFO, while his mother, from an immigrant background, worked as an accountant.

System Context

This shift in their financial landscape coincides with Sofia's desire for more living space for their family. Although this might not appear as a specific transition, it did seem as though they would be shifting in lifestyle. Their moving from an apartment to a home in Riverdale or Westchester would represent a financial change. However, Bogdan's parents have not been entirely forthcoming about the trust's terms, leading to confusion and hesitance about making decisions. Despite having diligently managed their budget and savings over the past twelve years, concerns linger about family housing ownership. Bogdan's parents clearly stated that the trust money would be in Bogdan's name, raising questions about property ownership if they were to purchase a house. In addition, his parents were "were weighing in" on cost of housing. All this fed into Bogdan's own ambivalence about the move.

Their earlier experience buying a home in Upstate New York during Covid was marked by anxiety for Bogdan, who likened the property to a "ball and chain." The topic of home ownership is thus fraught with tension.

Their previous couple's therapist had labeled it a "lifestyle difference," but we aimed to explore the underlying meanings it held for each of them. It was an opportunity to help them understand what kind of family environment they would want to create for their growing family. The issues for this transition encompass the money side of it as well as the relational side. The financial side required more clarity as to the principle amount and who and how it could get used. On the relational side we needed more clarity regarding the potential final shift to their family life together and how they wanted to shape that.

Treatment

As we delved into these issues, I sensed that the potential financial gift was unsettling their equilibrium. At other moments, I wondered if the opposite might be true. Was there always this uneasiness in the relational dynamic? This financial uncertainty led us to uncover relational dynamics that had been brewing over the years. Sofia expressed feelings of loneliness and invisibility. Bogdan's work-at-home setup, which limited his social interactions to virtual meetings and family time, left little time for them as a couple. Their exchanges had largely centered around co-parenting, leaving little room for nurturing their relationship. I aimed to help them rebuild the foundation of their partnership.

Recognizing the intersection between money and their couple's dynamic, I proposed a values exercise as described in Chapter 4. This could potentially lead to a "five-year family plan." It would allow us to identify areas of alignment and divergence in their goals and aspirations for their lives. Together, they discovered agreement on broad topics such as education, travel, and cultural experiences. Reviewing their annual budget revealed pleasant surprises in terms of financial transparency and collaborative management.

However, we identified one significant misalignment: their views on family housing. Sofia envisioned a family home as a supportive sanctuary with private spaces for each member, while Bogdan viewed a house merely as physical space. To further explore this, I encouraged them to look at potential homes together, which led to a practical exercise highlighting their differing emotional perspectives. As Bogdan expressed his anxieties, Sofia shared her desire for a stable home environment, stemming from her own childhood of frequent relocations.

Over the following months, we oscillated between addressing financial concerns and relationship dynamics, exploring the deeper meanings behind their feelings. Discussions about Bogdan's relationship with his parents illuminated triggers that fueled his anxiety and clouded his perspective on facts. At the same time, Sofia acknowledged her feelings of sadness and loneliness, linking them to a pattern of decision-making rooted in her family of origin, where she often assumed the "parentified" child role.

Throughout our sessions, we toggled between practical discussions and emotional explorations, which worked effectively for both Bogdan and Sofia. Using business terminology resonated with Bogdan, particularly when discussing Sofia's loneliness in her parenting role as she navigated school choices for their eldest child. It became evident that Sofia was acting as the "general," directing the logistics while Bogdan supported implementation. I introduced the concept of needing a "thought partner," drawing parallels to strategic planning, which ultimately led to a breakthrough in their conversations. Our time together focused on their dynamic and how we might shift that for each of them. The discussions brought them to a different level of understanding each other.

By consistently prioritizing their marriage over financial discussions, we uncovered layers within their relationship that stemmed from deep-seated dependencies and traditional roles.

Treatment Outcome

As a result of our work, Sofia and Bogdan successfully moved into a new home and transformed their marital relationship, fostering a partnership that brought them mutual comfort and satisfaction. Bogdan made significant efforts to develop his "empathy muscle," while Sofia looked forward to more date nights and intimate moments.

They understood that the road ahead would not always be smooth but were grateful for the changes that they had worked to accomplish. The issue of the money led us to a more complex landscape of the couple's dynamic.

10.3 Yumi

Initial intake and Presenting Problem

Yumi reached out to me via email. She reminded me that she and her ex-husband had seen us through the money and family life project in 2010 for consultation. She said she needed a therapist and would I consider seeing her. Her presenting problem was her relationship with her daughter, Grace. After the divorce in 2010, her ex-husband had sued her twice. She had moved to a smaller apartment and 2016 Grace had gone to live with Eric, her ex-husband. She and Grace had been estranged for many years since then. Grace had just started college and Yumi thought this might be a good time to work on reconciliation. During Covid her son Nathan had lived with her and Grace had lived with Eric. During that time, they acted like a family unit, more than at any other time. Their boundaries had dissolved.

Family Membership

Yumi, a Korean-American woman aged 60, and Eric, a Korean-American man aged 61, were divorced in 2010. It was very contentious, and there were lawsuits following the divorce. They had two children, Nathan, aged 25, and Grace, aged 21. There are no living grandparents. Yumi has an older sister and younger brother. I have no information for Eric's side of the family.

System Context

Divorce is a multidimensional process. From a legal and social status perspective, it is an event. It moves people from being married legally to being legally divorced. It shifts the financial picture for each member of the couple and potentially for the children. From a family systems perspective, divorce is a process of family change. The family continues in a different form. Each family member will be profoundly affected by the divorce. Each one will have to learn new ways of coping and relating to each other. The divorcing process culminates in a complex redefinition of relationships within the family.

This transition most often intersects with a developmental transition, sometimes causing interruption to one or the other. For instance, the divorce seemed to intersect with the the launching of the couple's young adults. The stress of divorce ranks high on the list of stressful life events. Normal coping abilities are taxed by complex personal and familial changes. Everyone in the family faces these challenges. The objectives are threefold: the family remains a family in a new form; negative impact for children is minimized; and both ex-spouses integrate the divorce into their lives in a healthy way.

As we began, Yumi shared parts of her story. It appeared to me that neither she nor Eric had completed their emotional divorce. Nor had they completed the financial side. During Covid they spent lots of time together as a family. Grace kept her distance from Yumi. They still owned commercial space together. Their lives appeared to be intertwined. If Yumi didn't feel well, she called Eric. They were still in conflict over child support. This was ten years post legal divorce, and yet it sounded to me as though Yumi had multiple issues to work on in treatment. These appeared to be her emotional divorce from Eric; her relationship with her daughter; and her anxiety related to financial stability. Our work would require a complex multilevel approach.

Treatment

During the very first meetings with Yumi, I mostly listened and commented when I thought I could be heard. Yumi's anxiety was quite high, and it manifested in her talking continuously. The three issues that surfaced continuously: her relationship to Grace, her relationship to Eric, and her anxiety about her financial future.

By this time, Grace was away in college. Initially, I guided her to stay connected to her daughter in whatever way she could. I suggested she contact her consistently and not react to any lack of reciprocity. I reminded her that college is its own world, and phone calls from the outside can sometimes feel disruptive. She was able to hear that, maintain a connection, and acknowledge the positive impact when they actually had a conversation. There was a continuous consistent trend line in a slight upward motion. As in anything, we managed the setbacks.

As Yumi revealed her relationship to Eric, it appeared to be much more complex. Her family history revealed a mother who was mostly absent emotionally and physically and her father, who was a fun-loving person but provided little guidance for Yumi and her siblings. She had met Eric soon after she had started her small business. He fostered her dependency by helping her with all challenges and taking care of her in small incremental ways. He was doing things for her that she had never experienced in her homelife with her parents. As their life progressed, Eric would also become judgmental and impose edicts for her. It sounded as though he fostered her dependency and at the same time undermined her sense of self. When her children were young and she wanted to spend more time with them, Eric would insist that she go to work. Her small business had become quite successful and was providing a good lifestyle for their family. She felt both trapped in their marriage and yet so dependent on his care. At some stage, their sex life dwindled, and Eric decided that they needed to invite others in. It would stimulate their sexual connection. This became the beginning of the end of their marriage. Yumi had an affair with someone, Eric discovered it, and wrote to the man's wife. This ended the affair as well as the marriage without real resolution of Yumi's attachment to Eric or Eric's to Yumi.

Throughout the course of treatment, we worked on Yumi being able to understand her emotional dependency on Eric. Initially, I would comment on Yumi's fear of Eric. Then I would alert her to her need for him, especially if she was feeling vulnerable because she was sick or conflicted as to how to solve a problem. This continued for a while as Yumi vacillated herself between feeling intimidated and dependent. She asked, "why can I not let go of this person?" Overtime, she began to shift to see him in his attempts to control a situation. She began to stop answering his calls and the more she did that, the more he called. She began to recognize this behavior as his need to know what was happening to stay in control. His words did not always match his deeds. Overtime, Yumi developed a more definitive boundary for herself. She stopped calling him for "help." She stopped asking him about their daughter. She started living her life. She got herself a cat from ASPCA which gave her someone to care for. She began cooking for herself. All these things added up to her taking care of herself. When she was diagnosed with a chronic disease that required consistent treatment, she did her due diligence thoroughly and managed her care. She began to appreciate that her resourcefulness that she manifested in her small business could be directed toward herself to give her the internal fortitude for this phase of her life.

The third issue that has been consistent throughout is the completion of their business divorce. When they divorced fourteen years ago, they owned the commercial property together that housed both of their businesses. They had a separate amendment to the divorce to define clearly how the property should be sold. Post Covid Eric determined that he no longer required the space and told Yumi numerous times that he wants to put the property on the market. Yumi's entire business is housed in a part of the space and because she does production that requires tools, machines, etc. The move for her could be quite costly. Initially, I was able to ask her what her options might look like if the property were sold. I asked her to do an exercise of defining the options and the implications for each. This is where I actually use my own business knowledge to try to move her forward. The last thing she wants is another lawsuit with Eric. At one point I refer her to a business colleague to help her with the potential financial picture to determine if she could buy Eric's share. Here we are dealing with a financial reality and Yumi's survival anxiety. Her business is her means of support. She bridles, and delays talking to real estate brokers. She puts up hurdles at every turn. She prolongs and procrastinates, and Eric gets more and more frustrated. She begins to understand that her business life will not have to stop. She goes over her financial circumstances with her financial advisor. She begins to understand that her work might take a different "form." She even ponders that perhaps she's ready to give up the day-to-day responsibility of business ownership. She finds a broker and they are able to move forward with putting the space on the market. Yumi has trouble dealing with the ambiguity of the situation. That said she understands the financial implications. We are now able to talk about the meaning of all this for her . . . her survival anxiety which manifests in her working 24/7; her need to have everything buttoned up before she can make a decision; and her inability to trust her own decision-making.

This phase of our work required attention to the very practical business side of Yumi's life. We had to talk "business concepts" and use financial data to tease out what was potentially the risks for Yumi's work life moving forward.

Change to Date

Yumi has moved further in detaching from Eric and connecting to both her children. She rarely speaks to Eric unless it relates to "family planning." Both children had graduations late Spring, and Yumi structured both weekends for herself and their family so that they could be together but maintain the boundaries. These graduations went smoothly. The experience taught Yumi how important it is for her to plan ahead for family vacations with her children as well as holidays. The family is finally moving into a new form and both young adult children are recognizing the shift. Yumi and Grace talk frequently, and slowly Yumi is becoming a more significant emotional resource to her daughter. The third objective is moving at a slower pace. The property will go onto the market in January. We continue to follow the money to understand the level of Yumi's anxiety and determine the meaning for her. From a family perspective, the family has moved to its new form. Yumi is learning how to parent young adult children.

10.4 Doug and His Daughter Eliana

Initial Contact

Doug reached out to me with an email requesting a time for him and his adult single daughter to meet with me. He asked if I might be available to mediate a few conversations between him and his 31-year-old daughter, regarding some difficulty they are having communicating about a change in his financial support for her. He continued to expand that it was in the context of his impending remarriage. I agreed to set a Zoom meeting with each of them separately before agreeing to anything else.

Presenting Problem

In my initial separate conversations with Doug and his daughter Eliana, I identified two or three issues that required attention and were potentially problematic. First and foremost, I learned that Doug and his ex-wife had been divorced for five plus years. During that time, Doug continued to support his two adult daughters. Neither daughter was working in areas that brought them any income. Eliana had recently graduated from acupuncture school and was starting her own practice. Neither Doug nor his ex-wife Susan had ever talked to their daughters about financial matters or financial responsibility. This seemed strange to me as the daughters were young adults, well beyond the age whereby parents would be sole support.

The second issue that got a "flag" for me was Doug's timing. He was about to get remarried and very much wanted his daughters to be there. He was pressuring for this conversation to take place ASAP so they could put it to rest. He denied any financial connection between the lowering of his daughter's allowance and his new marriage.

What I also discovered in my conversation with Eliana was that Doug had never sat down with her to talk about her plan for financial independence. He had merely told her in an email that he was going to sequentially over a year lower the amount of money he would be sending her. He had provided no guidance. Both the timing around the wedding and Doug's communication choice were the other issues that promoted my warning signs.

System Context

As this story unfolded, the launching phase became my frame of reference. The initial stage of launching requires a continuous separation process. It appeared that Eliana was in the second launching phase where she was establishing her work foundation as well as her relational one. The area around financial independence, as well as parents' readiness to transfer financial responsibility appeared incomplete. What I discovered in my conversation with Eliana was that her father had never sat her down or "taken her to lunch" to have the financial independence conversation. He had made an edict and refused to engage in any conversation. He cited his objectives around initiating this. It all related to financial independence. In addition, Dad had moved out of State to live with his future wife and her children. For some reason, Doug did not see any connection with the timing of his decision to lower the allowance and the remarriage. His daughter did. Eliana expressed concern about his connection to this new family and what it might mean for her and her sister. These were the issues that became highlighted for me and required some exploration to understand what it all meant to each of them. There were lots of emotional undertones. The challenge was how to proceed.

Family Membership

The nuclear family consisted of Doug, a white Jewish male, 64 years old, and his ex-wife Susan, an Asian female 60 years old. They had two biracial daughters ages 28 and 31. Eliana, the eldest, had just graduated from professional acupuncture school, and Adrianna was a documentary film maker. The remarriage was Doug's third marriage. His future wife had two college aged children. Doug had been the primary provider in his family. He had developed a successful consulting practice in the business world. Susan had worked initially but stopped many years ago. Eliana was just starting to build a private practice. Doug's future wife had an academic career.

Treatment

After talking with both Doug and Eliana individually, I set a time to talk together. There was lots of tension, and I began to realize that I had done this too quickly, having been influenced by Doug and his pressure of time. As Eliana said, her father had his vision of how things should be but had never engaged her in that conversation. She was feeling unsupported in the launching of her new practice. She agreed with the concept of her becoming financially self-sustaining but viewed the edict as unilateral and unaccommodating. We ended the session on a better note as I had engaged Eliana to find out her "business plan" for launching her practice. That said, I asked for the next session to meet with Doug alone. He was reluctant as he thought we were there to mediate. I suggested I needed some clarification to proceed. I also reiterated that I viewed my role as facilitator not mediator. I suggested to him that my work would assist them in having a conversation about the financial issues as well as the emotional ones. He was not pleased with my perspective. I then turned our conversation to explore how he and Susan had tried to teach his daughters about money. I asked if they as a family talked about money. I used as a frame the partnership questions that we use at the beginning of our workshop. I just touched on his experience during his young adult years. He said he had been "thrown into the waters." He translated this by telling me how his parents had just cut him off financially when he finished his education.

In my second individual time with Doug, I asked him how he had presented this idea to Eliana. He said he had sent her a very long email sharing his thoughts and his plan. I wondered aloud why he had done this via email and not in person. He said he thought that was the best format for his telling her without interruption.

I wondered why he was so hesitant to have the conversation.

Following that conversation, Eliana reached out to ask if she might talk to me briefly. Her message to me was stunning as well as informational. Her Dad had sent her an email questioning my competence. He sighted the awkwardness he experienced in our first joint conversation. Eliana said this was not unusual for him to do. She felt as though he were laying the groundwork to not continue working with me and coopting her to join him in that decision. She was saddened by this as she had experienced our brief work as helpful to her. I suggested she speak with him and say that he needed to raise these issues with me in our next meeting.

That did happen, and we talked about it. Our conclusion was to terminate our work together. I realized that he was not available and his attempt to discredit me would forever sabotage the work. I offered each of them an opportunity to talk with me. Eliana did take me up on that and I just gave her some suggestions as to how she might engage with him around the finances. She understood him better than I had.

Reflections

Initially, in my mind, I categorized this case as a short-term facilitation between father and daughter. When Eliana called to share the email her father had sent, I realized that Doug had agreed to see me for his primary agenda, to resolve his decision about the money and get Eliana to come to the wedding. He thought this could happen in two–three sessions., a more transactional approach. Where did I go wrong? Often the work I do in this area crosses between consulting and therapy. Over the years, I have come to recognize that I must be clear in my head as to which hat I am wearing. I too was coopted by Doug's belief that our work could be short term. As I mulled over this situation, I realized that I did not do a more thorough due diligence in the initial stage of engagement.

10.5 Jean

Initial Contact and Presenting Problem

Jean emailed me requesting an appointment time. She had gotten my contact from a friend who thought I could be helpful. Our initial session was on Zoom as we were mid pandemic. Jean explained that her law firm had mandatory retirement, and she was close to her date. It was making her very anxious. She hadn't really put any thought to her future life. She was still working as if she were just starting out. Her objective in calling me was to be intentional about this next phase of her life. "I've got to take care of myself. I want to do what I enjoy doing." Her calendar was filled daily. She needed help with this life transition.

Family Membership

Jean had been married to Charles for thirty years. They had separated about ten years ago but agreed not to get legally divorced. They had two biological adult children and one adult child they had raised, the son of Charles' sister. His parents had died in a car accident. No one was married yet. Jean had met Saif a year ago, and he had moved into her apartment. She was enjoying that relationship and looked forward to it continuing. He had three adult children. Jean went on to describe her family of origin. Both her parents were deceased. They had divorced several years after she and her six siblings had left home. In her family, Jean was the only college graduate who had gone onto a professional career. She was the "hero child." Both parents had become part of Alcoholic Anonymous groups, and Jean had been a long-time participant in Alanon. She described her siblings as caught in the old family drama. She helped each one in different ways.

System Context

Retirement, no matter the age at which it happens, requires planning both personally and financially. As in other transitions, there is a systemic impact. Key considerations include financial security, healthcare needs, lifestyle changes, potential for a new purpose, managing your time, maintaining social connections, and ensuring your estate planning is in order; essentially, planning for a stable income stream, managing potential healthcare costs, and figuring out how to fill your days with meaningful activities while adapting to a new routine without the structure of work. Changes in these areas effect one's relationships and so I considered where to start. Jean took the lead and started to talk about her work life balance. She called herself a workaholic and noted that for her entire career she had pushed hard. Her motivations had been to never be dependent on a man and give her children economic security. She knew she had accomplished her first goal. She wasn't so sure of the second. Here was an opening to discuss her financial plans. I asked her what planning she had done. She responded, "like Scarlett O'Hara, my mantra has always been, I'll deal with it tomorrow." She continued with, "I hate talking about money . . . it makes me very uncomfortable!!" I wondered what the underlying emotions might be for her. I thought about how we might help her shed this discomfort.

Treatment

Because Jean had brought up the financial issue, it provided easy access for us to talk about it. She described how she had spent decades in "survival mode" and now was feeling overwhelmed and extremely self-critical. Saif stepped in and made her a spreadsheet on her computer. She claimed that every time she opened it, it all felt unmanageable to her. She was having trouble processing the information in front of her. She went on to claim that it was just "another fucking thing" she had to deal with, claiming again how much she hated talking about money!" I chose this time to begin to explore with Jean what this very strong reaction to money was all about. She said that growing up in her family her parents were always worrying about money. Both were alcoholics. This manifested in different ways. Her father always spent too much money gambling leaving little for the family needs. Her mother worried daily over how to feed and dress the family. As the oldest, Jean had been caught in the middle of their arguments, trying desperately to hold the family together. She had always felt like she had to fix it! Her solution had always been to make a lot of money! That was all she needed to do! That was her solution to the family trauma! Our time was coming to an end, and I decided to let this conversation percolate until next time.

As treatment progressed, there were times when Jean would come to a session with collateral issues relating to her children, her work, her relationship to Saif. When there was an opening to the finances, I usually took it and asked her how she was doing in that realm. She often responded by saying, "I'm creating this problem. My denial, my discomfort, my judgment, all are getting in my way to begin to look at my financial situation." I responded by asking, "What do you believe might be helpful to break through that?"

Jean understood that clarity on her future life choices would be contingent on this financial knowledge and yet she was emotionally blocking access. She said that talking about money and all these associations she had with it was proving to be good. She could feel herself shedding some of the "voices of despair."

During this time Saif was working on his own potential retirement as well. His "nut"/net worth was not as much as Jean's. He talked about moving out of the city. He enjoyed physical activity and explored communities in the South. Although Jean would always join him, she found nothing that resonated with her. What this also showed her was that her big fear of ending up a "bag lady" was probably completely out of the bounds of her reality. The relational context served her well as Saif was always talking about "the money." She loved him and wanted him to become her life partner. She understood that she had to work through her denial and resistance around money!

Shortly after this recognition, Jean attended a family event, her niece's eighteenth birthday celebration. She talked about the difference in dress code and speech patterns. She shared how she became acutely aware of these things that day. She and Saif had talked about it on their ride back to the city. Saif had suggested the concept of class difference, something that had never surfaced for her before. Something that resonated so clearly for her! I suggested that we do a money-focused genogram of her family. I explained that this might help her see the patterns more distinctly. She agreed.

It is very useful to do a money/class focused genogram with a client. The graphic of seeing the family in this way often triggers a "light bulb" moment.

This is what happened with Jean. As we developed the genogram together, she began to see how she had gotten stuck in her family of origin's patterns around money. It also showed her how she had moved up in the socio-economic class structure but was still maintaining a "poverty mentality."

This became a turning point for Jean. She recognized her fear of "financial ruin," her childlike reactions to adult problems. Her lifelong disappointment and recognition that no one was there to take care of her. She noted how these fears had motivated her to work more. Work had become her means of survival. Work has become her solution in managing her money anxieties. Paradoxically, her "working class mentality around money" coupled with the underlying shame had propelled her to become a workaholic. These same issues were now preventing her from her financial planning. This connection that she made led to opening the door and her beginning to understand and deal with her financial picture.

Her initial step was to call her accountant. She had to get some tax information together for the IRS. She had to get her "house in order." She was finally moving forward on the financial issues.

For the remainder of Jean's treatment, we continued to deal with her financial picture. We were also able to discuss the relational expectations for her and Saif with their respective children, who were all adults. She was able to write a letter to the executive committee of her law firm about her retirement. She became more pragmatic and less afraid. She hired a financial advisor as she understood her own limitations. She was on her way to retirement.

Treatment Outcome

As a result of our work together, Jean started making her retirement plans. In addition to her financial planning, she also shifted her relationships with her adult children, recognizing them as adults who had already begun to make their choices both professionally and relationally. She cut back on her work schedule from five days to three and decided to only work with present and historic clients. She said to me, "I'm ready!" She is working on this next phase of her life. She is able to manage her anxiety moments and reference herself back to our work together.

Addendum

The money-focused genogram proved to be a good turning point for her. We had laid enough of the foundation to enable her to be available and present when we drew it together. It was helpful to use a big pad so we both could manage the process together. Please reference chapter 6.

10.6 Leslie and Greg

Initial Contact

Leslie and Greg requested therapy at the Ackerman clinic. Because one of the issues they cited in the intake process was money, the case was referred to our project. When I received the paperwork, the money issue was quite ambiguous. We decided to see them for an initial interview to assess more deeply. I called to set a time and introduced the parameters of the research, which included taping of our sessions, permission to use tapes for professional teaching and understanding that a colleague would be watching behind the one-way mirror. They agreed to all.

Presenting Problem

I ushered Leslie, a White woman aged sixty-four, and Greg, a White man, age sixty-five, into the studio at Ackerman. Both had been professionals in the marketing industry. Neither was working. They lived in Brooklyn and basically said, "everything is screwed up in our lives." They went on to describe a myriad of problems. Greg had had a bout with cancer. Both his parents had died, and he and his sister had been in high conflict around the estate. Leslie had written a book but had put her marketing agenda on hold. Greg was encouraging her to do it. I wondered how they filled their time. Greg then told me that they rented out the second bedroom in their rented apartment through Airbnb and so their time was spent either talking to guests, cleaning up, etc. Since they had presented money as an issue in their intake, I used that opening to ask questions about their finances. Greg answered with lots of ambiguity. Our time was just about up, and so I asked if they could please work on their monthly budget and bring it to our next meeting. This was my attempt to better understand their financial situation. I purposely did not give any specific guidelines as it seemed that Greg would understand full well what I was asking for. When working with couples, I usually ask them to sit together to do this.

Family Membership

Leslie and Greg had been together for over twenty years. They had never formally married nor were there any offspring from either partner. Greg had a sister who he claimed was emotionally unstable. Both of his parents had died in the past decade. Leslie has a brother who lives in NYC. Her parents were deceased as well. Both had had careers in marketing. Greg had a consulting business which he had sold many years ago. The genogram felt quite sparse.

System Context

Here was a white middle-class couple; both had had professional careers. It appeared that they might be transitioning to retirement. They presented visually as a couple who managed okay. They lived in a popular neighborhood in Brooklyn. Their apartment was a floor in a brownstone. There appeared to be medical issues, legal issues and as a result financial issue. Greg had had a few bouts with cancer, and Leslie described how she had been his advocate and caregiver. Greg described his sister who had "stolen" his parents' property after their death. He had been in/out of court system now for many years. This dissonance between visual and historic information alongside their comment that "everything is screwed up in our lives" was quite stunning.

Treatment

Greg sat down and pulled out his papers as we began our second meeting. Leslie sat by him quietly. Greg started by showing me a briefing booklet he had prepared for how he might rejoin the marketing world. It took me a moment to register what he was showing me. He had developed a business plan rather then a household budget. I quickly responded with "I think you might have misunderstood what I had requested." I then suggested that we could gather the information now. I was determined to untangle what was happening here, and I thought the numbers would help to tell the story. I began collecting information about the expense side first. I asked about how much rent they paid; what were their utilities; cell phones; food and supplies; clothing; medical; and miscellaneous. One can discover a lot about a person/couple in just understanding the expenses in these different categories. While I was asking, I wrote down the numbers and calculated in my head the broad amount. I then went onto the income side. Leslie sat by Greg's side not really participating. Greg responded that most of their income came from renting the second bedroom through Airbnb. He was proud of feedback they got on the Airbnb website. They were considered very good hosts! I asked on average how much he makes through the rentals. He cited a number below what I had deemed their expenses were. He then continued to say that he also borrowed on his credit card to day trade to make up the number they needed for their expenses. The reality of their dire financial state started to "seep in" for me. Because both of them were sitting there with no reaction, I just collected the remaining information. I acknowledged how difficult this must be for both of them.

Throughout the next few sessions, they both shared what life had been like. Greg had been diagnosed with cancer, and Lisa had nursed him through it. There had been lots of issues with the settlement around Greg's parents' estate and so most of that had dissipated. Because they were on Medicaid, they had difficulty getting medical appointments. Because I was seeing this couple with a colleague from the project, we discussed how to proceed.

We decided that both of them needed the space to talk about what life had been like. We also agreed that the direction we might take would be to explore work options going forward. We recognized that both Leslie and Greg were in "deep denial" of their financial circumstances. Greg was living "day to day," and Leslie was giving him that responsibility.

After a few weeks of reviewing the same issues, I asked if either one of them would like to have a session alone. Greg said he was ok and declined the offer. Leslie was eager to schedule a time to meet.

During my time with Leslie, I decided to try to understand from her how she understood what had happened here. Since this couple was not legally married, what was the connection that kept them together? Leslie said that she loved Greg. They had been together for many years. She had taken care of him during his cancer treatment. She also realized that there was very little that connected them other then their history. In her mind, taking care of their finances would make him feel good and give them that connection. As I heard her, I ruminated about the connection and its meaning that she was describing. Was this about her desire to be cared for or his need to feel connected and proud? It was clear that they had both engaged in this relational premise of social gendered roles. This had become their bond.

We decided to continue seeing them together, and our discussions became their day-to-day issues as well as potential work areas to explore. In addition, we were just at the initial "beta" stage of doing our workshops. I invited Leslie to become a participant. She jumped at the opportunity. It was very helpful for her.

During one of our sessions together, Leslie mentioned her desire to move to Arizona. I wondered how Greg felt about that. It was unclear to him, how they could make that happen. In that same session, Leslie mentioned that her birthday was coming up. I wished her well and asked how old she was. She said it was a big birthday . . . she was turning 65. I immediately asked her if she had looked into social security.

This led to Leslie exploring her options for collecting social security and what that would mean. It also prompted Greg to look into his options. It opened up an avenue for them to begin to plan a move out west, something she had wanted to do for a long time.

Outcome

Leslie and Greg were able to get enough funds together to move out west. It took a while for Greg to get "on board" with the idea. Leslie had said she was going with or without him! They did move right before the pandemic. Months later, Leslie wrote to me to thank me and let me know that they had landed in a good place. Greg had been able to find some consulting work, and she was working part-time.

I recently reached out to see how they were doing. I told her about this book and just asked her to give some feedback. Here's what she wrote.

> I realize G will never change. He just can't get beyond that wall. You helped me see that wall even though he couldn't. So I need to accept and navigate my own inner universe to get where I want to go. When you've been a caregiver your entire life, focusing on yourself feels unfamiliar. Women truly need support to learn to care about themselves first, particularly when establishing their financial freedom. The system doesn't want us independent. G has been working with small local companies doing marketing. He could be doing better and more if he'd listen to me but well, you know how that goes. I was working in an art gallery for almost a year which was stabilizing and interesting while I was building a new website for my Wisdom keeping courses, which I'm still working on. But I shattered my elbow hiking in April and had major surgery. I've recovered better than expected and will have the plate and screws taken out in January. Will be pretty much back to normal which is a miracle. In the process, I began creating art, which I call Frequency Art. I've been receiving a lot of interest from people, so will start selling prints early next year. I did art as a child. It was the first thing I wanted to be. And honestly, the only thing I chose. Everything else chose me. I'm happily having an art exhibit here in the spring. Who would have thought! I am grateful for your grounding and focus during a very unstable and chaotic time in my life. I'm still physically and emotionally recovering. What I loved most about your class is that it illuminated things I hadn't thought about and if you can't see them, you can't change them. I am all about making the unconscious conscious and you have a gentle gift for that. The class made me feel stronger than I felt at that time. I wish I had met you 30 years ago! Let me know if I can offer any other info to you.

10.7 Genevieve and Bill

Initial Contact

Genevive called with trepidation in her voice. Rather than introduce herself initially, she started talking about her crisis state. Bill, her husband of over 40 years, had asked for a divorce. This came as quite a shock to her. She was feeling quite anxious all the time, unable to sleep, and her good friend suggested she call me. It was clear to me from our two-minute conversation that my best next step would be to offer her an appointment as soon as possible. I bypassed my usual questions, acknowledged her state, and asked if she were free to come the next day. She said yes, thanked me and said she felt some relief already.

Presenting Problem

Genevieve presented as a Caucasian woman of French-Canadian descent. She had met her husband many years ago when she was working as an airline stewardess. He was an entrepreneur and had become quite successful. She told me that they had tried to have children unsuccessfully. Their life had revolved mostly around Bill's schedule, which included his business commitments as well as his philanthropic ones. The picture she was projecting was one of "dutiful wife." She was completely confused by Bill's request to get divorced. Genevieve, as she liked to be called, described how the last ten years of their marriage had become "flat," but she assumed that was "normal" for their stage of life. As she told me her story, I was able to understand more about their lifestyle and interaction. I listened and left space for Genevieve to talk as much as she had to. I realized that she had not shared this much detail about her life with anyone. Although she might have been feeling a sense of relief, I also did not want her to walk away feeling "overly exposed" so I listened mostly. As she commented, she has always been a private person.

The Family Membership

By the end of our first session, I got a sense of Genevieve and Bill's limited social and family network. Although Genevieve had six siblings, they all lived in Canada and were older. She did mention that Bill had nieces whom they saw regularly. I was also was confused by her description of Bill's behavior. She used the word erratic. She alluded to an indecisiveness that had never been there before. I asked if she thought it might be helpful for Bill to come in for a session to help me better appreciate what was happening between them. She did not know if he would do that, but she agreed that it would be helpful.

System Context

When divorce after 40+ years of marriage occurs, it is imperative to understand what is happening for both parties. When a couple has been together for that long, there is so much life/history they have had together. One must wonder what is happening in the system to trigger a breakup. Is it something that one person has been "hiding" for a long time? Is it a long-term affair that one partner has been having or is it an apathy that has settled into the system? Is the life transition of adjustment to retirement an issue? These were the questions cropping up in my mind. Genevieve had talked about her anger at Bill for never really treating her like a partner. They had a long history of sexual problems. She also shared how anxious Bill was about aging. She commented that her head knew she could take care of herself, but in her heart, she was scared for him as she thought someone could take advantage of him. As I thought about all these issues, I understood why I had intuitively suggested that Bill come for our next session. It is informative to see both individuals, sometimes together and sometimes individually. The information and often differing perspectives give you more information for your developing systemic hypothesis. I was pleased when I got the email from Genevieve confirming Bill would attend our next session.

In that session when Bill came with Genevieve, I discovered that Bill had asked Genevieve for a temporary separation. He reassured her about her financial situation. They talked about their multiple residences. And I learned about a strong connection they both had to a university in the Midwest. Bill was connected to the sport teams and coaches, and Genevieve was involved with the museum. This was where most of their philanthropic energies landed. And this was where Bill became energized and engaged. This connection in essence seemed to have replaced his business activities which had narrowed down to participation on business boards. By the end of our time together, I heard from Bill how he felt a separation would be best. He had made his decision. No one was going to change his mind! For Genevieve, she ended by stating: "I trusted him, saw strength in him. He's good and kind. But I'm angry as he does not respect or love me."

Beginning Stage of Treatment

For the next month, Genevieve came to see me. Genevieve and Bill began to live separately. She kept saying how angry she was, and then she would say, "I also keep thinking that he's doing things that don't make sense." For instance, she commented that she had all his medical information and understood his complete medical "resume." When he switched all his doctors to the Mid-West University Hospital, it did not make sense. This is not where we live and none of them have the medical history. "I don't understand why he's doing this." This prompted me to wonder what was going on with Bill. Was he blocking Genevieve out? Was he attempting to shift because of his personal connections? Did he think he'd get good care as a result now that

Genevieve might be "out of the picture?" I held back from asking if he had ever seen a neurologist as Genevieve also described his inability sometimes to remember where he was; his confusion with money and payments and his erratic decision-making. Was the change in his mind related to their separation?

Going back to the presenting problem of divorce, I wondered again how much Bill had reflected on what this separation would look like. I detected some impulsivity on his part. Throughout my years of practice, I have taken a two-pronged approach. I allow for lots of expression of the inherent ambivalence around the divorcing process. While I surface and process the ambivalence, at the same time, I encourage envisioning the future and understanding what it might look like. I often suggest consultation with a lawyer or two to understand the practical side of divorce. I present the concept that divorce includes both an emotional divorce as well as a business divorce. Within this conversation, the money issue surfaces readily. It is here that one can raise the money issue and discover roles and responsibilities of each partner. This intervention expands one's understanding of the couple's dynamic, especially around money. In addition, it gives you a window into understanding how much each client understands the couple's financial picture.

In Genevieve and Bill's story, it became clear that Genevieve had become Bill's caretaker while Bill was the provider. They never sat together to discuss their financial state. Although Genevieve had paid household bills, the bigger financial picture appeared to be Bill's realm of responsibility. They were not big spenders, and as Bill had reassured Genevieve in our session, there were plenty of assets for them each to maintain the quality of life they had enjoyed. The open question was how their finances might get divided and then how would Genevieve manage. Although she had taken care of day-to-day running of households, she did not have a concept of the larger picture, that is, category of assets, investments, cost of operating the small plane they owned, and philanthropic information. It became clear that Genevieve eventually would require education in these areas.

These are things that would be raised by her lawyer eventually, but warrant mentioning during our conversations. As a therapist, I try to ensure that the client has the financial understanding of what their future will look like and how they will be able to manage. As therapist, one must be comfortable with this information. It is here that the tools we used in the workshop like the values cards, or the money-focused genogram can be useful (chapters 4 and 6) for work with a client. In Genevieve's case it became helpful to have her identify what her priorities would be, especially once she had a divorce agreement and would have responsibilities that she had never had before.

We also used a money-focused genogram to understand the family messages around money. As she began to appreciate her new responsibilities, would they be contradictory to the family premises around money? It is also useful to review your own knowledge and comfort around financial data.

Change during Treatment

Bill and Genevieve lived separately for three months and then Bill would begin to make overtures to Genevieve to go out to dinner. He would also call her in the evening saying he was lonely. Genevieve held to her ideas of how things between them would have to change. It took a while but eventually Genevieve agreed to have dinner with Bill. She began spending more time with him and came in saying that she was concerned there was something medically going on with Bill. The symptoms, similar to those she had talked about in our initial sessions, seemed to have become more pronounced. In the interim, Genevieve did finally go to see a lawyer who suggested she consider a post nuptial agreement rather than a separation agreement. This idea resonated with Genevieve because she felt that if there was something wrong health wise with Bill, she would want to be his caretaker. She also required the security that a post nuptial agreement would offer in case he became erratic again and requested a divorce. During this time, she also insisted that he see a neurologist. As suspected, Bill was diagnosed with MCI and put on medication. So, eventually, our work took a turn from the possibility of divorce to helping Genevieve reenter her life with Bill. Her challenge would be to sustain boundaries and maintain the independent projects she had started for herself. Overtime, Genevieve also very carefully took over their finances as Bill became less and less able to do that job.

This change shifted the objectives of our work together as Genevieve took on more and more financial responsibility. This was out of necessity as a result of Bill's condition. She did it cautiously and accessed outside advisors as she required more knowledge.

Treatment Outcome

Genevieve developed agency in multiple dimensions as she lived this last chapter with Bill. Her ability to make decisions relating to financial matters developed over time. She was able to shape her life according to her values. She enhanced her familial relationships with Bill's nieces as well as her remaining siblings. She became adept at using financial advisors incorporating her knowledge as well as her intuition. Bill did pass away but was very well taken care of by Genevieve, and by that time, Genevieve was also quite prepared to manage her life and her wealth. As a result of the work, we did together in preparing Genevieve for the eventual outcome, she was able to develop agency and feel more competent and qualified to actually take on the responsibilities.

10.8 Desmond and Michelle

Initial Contact and Presenting Problem

As part of the research project, we continue to see couples who present with financial issues through the clinic at the Ackerman Institute. The intake coordinator reached out to me about Desmond and Michelle. The intake sheet described an African-American couple, ages fifty-seven and forty-eight respectively, married fifteen years. They had no children. Their presenting problem was lots of tension and fighting in their home. The immediate pressure was stated as job loss. In that first meeting, we discovered that this was the third job loss for Desmond in the past decade. Michelle was quite concerned about their financial situation. She had no details as Desmond managed everything. She also described his drinking and marijuana use as becoming problematic and wondered if this was affecting his work habits. Desmond described Michelle as being abusive and constantly "on his back" to do everything for her.

Family Membership

As their story unfolded, we discovered that Desmond was one of four children. He was the only child in his family to have both a college and graduate degree. He had a work history in substantial financial service companies. He had been married and divorced, no children. His father was a college graduate and served as a state senator for many years. His mother was a "stay at home" Mom who taught him and his three younger brothers discipline. He was her favorite but only when he performed well. Both parents were deceased. Michelle on the other hand grew up in an abusive household. Her father, an alcoholic, was rarely home, and her mother became quite abusive both emotionally and physically with her and her younger two sisters. Michelle had also been married and divorced, no children. In tracking work history, we discovered that Michelle had worked mostly temporary jobs. She was pursuing her bachelor's degree in social work. Desmond had a good work history up until his marriage to Michelle. He then began to have difficulty in the workplace. He blamed this last job loss on the constant financial pressure he was feeling from Michelle. He had been unable to meet her "inappropriate" expectations. She spent money without any discretion, and he was always trying to manage. (Because this couple presented with job loss as the issue, it became clear that we needed to do a money-focused genogram early on) These were some of the themes that surfaced.

System Context

In telling their story, it was apparent that the job loss had escalated the tension between Desmond and Michelle. The questions we pursued with them initially related to gathering the financial facts, that is, did they have savings and if so, how much? How would they be able to cover their monthly expenses? How long would that last? When an interruption like a job loss occurs, it is important to understand the immediate level of stress that the family/couple might be having. It became clear from the answers we were getting that Michelle was completely in the dark about their finances. Desmond answered most of our questions and even shared the debt they had accumulated, mostly credit card debt. The roles they had assumed around money became apparent with our questions and Michelle's facial expression as Desmond described the facts of their financial condition. She had never heard any of what Desmond was describing to us. It was clear that she had no sense of their financial circumstances. She had been totally in the dark when it came to finances. She had just spent without any frame of reference.

This job loss was clearly an interruption in their life cycle, which seemed to be exacerbating the ongoing tension in their marriage. This event had triggered an escalation in that tension. We determined that a shift in their financial partnership might alleviate some of that.

Treatment

We decided to address the job loss and the implications for that directly. At the end of our first meeting, we suggested that they sit down together to map out their financial plan for the next six–nine months. This was the time frame that Desmond thought he would need before getting his next job. Michelle commented that he'd avoid it. We explored with Desmond what he thought about her comment? He actually said he'd welcome the partnership. We wondered what would really happen and looked to our next meeting to understand more about their couple dynamic. Although this initial intervention dealt with financial matters, it also would address the nature of the couple's relationship around money.

In our follow-up meeting, we discovered that Desmond had offered multiple options for he and Michelle to meet to review their financial "state." For multiple reasons, Michelle could never make anytime work for her calendar. Finally, Desmond suggested that she set the time. She had too much schoolwork and put off their meeting. In their reporting this outcome, I wondered out loud what each one thought about this result. I noted that during our first meeting, the stress they cited around their finances appeared to be tremendous. I also remembered the relief that manifested when we suggested they sit down together to do this plan. Wondered if they had a perspective on what happened.

Michelle's response focused on what Desmond had not done for her all week, that is, walked the dog, helped with household. As a result, she didn't want to do this for him! I asked her why she thought sitting down to look at the finances meant doing something for him? I noted that I thought this job loss effected both their lives. I chose not to pursue further about the possible dynamic between them.

Desmond said he had a plan that he wanted to share with Michelle. He hoped that she would be ready to review it with him soon.

Our work then shifted to their interactive cycle, that is, the fighting and how that escalated. We began to understand the multiple meanings that shadowed these escalations. For one thing, I learned about the loss of the dream they had had together. The dream to have a family. They both acknowledged how deeply saddened they were to face that reality. In addition, they were both equally connected to "traditional" premises of gendered roles and responsibilities. We talked about the meanings of these defined roles. If Desmond was to be the provider, did that also mean he made all the final financial decisions. If so, what did that mean for Michelle. Was she willing to be totally dependent on Desmond for their sustainability? Could there be another way for them to think about this? Did this dynamic require such "rigidity" in their minds, or could they think about it with more flexibility? We discussed Desmond being the provider but there making joint decisions. We addressed how Desmond might help Michelle in maintaining their home. We wondered if they might be able to actually fix a budget and keep to it.

A few months into this process, Desmond began to move in his job search. He suggested that our conversations had helped him to move forward and understand that he potentially might have a partnership with Michelle that could fell less stressful!

Eventually, we went back to the financial plan as Desmond had laid it out. Michelle finally agreed to discuss it and began to take ownership of the plan by making suggestions and changes. She claimed that she did want to be a part of the decision-making.

Change as Result of Treatment

Eventually, Desmond was able to find a suitable job. They had been able to work together to get through that transition which became challenging financially. The fighting and tension diminished, and they began to enjoy life together socially. Michelle graduated with her bachelor's and began looking for a job. The shift in their dynamic from total dependency to more interdependence took time and effort on their part. They understood that the fighting was triggered by "not feeling cared for." They were able to see how that got translated into fights about money or "dog walking." Since they started operating as a team/partnership, all that had deescalated.

10.9 Tamera and Manuel

Initial Contact

Tamera wrote to say her therapist suggested she speak to someone specifically about money. She and her fiancé Manuel (Manny) were getting married in a few months and wanted to discuss a pre-nup agreement. She indicated that she was bringing in "family money" and that she was self-conscious, having never "talked numbers" with Manny. She said they had a great relationship, and she felt sure they could work it out, but that she felt stuck and would feel safer disclosing the dollar amounts with a coach/therapist present.

Presenting Problem

Tamera, twenty-eight, presented as a White woman born in Seattle. Manny, thirty, was born in Ecuador.

Tamera and her fiancé had met four years prior in graduate school, where she was studying law, and he was studying computer science. They bonded over a love of rock climbing and dedication to the environment. They both work in non-profits where they had nearly the same salary. They are both very hard-working and career-identified, though their life was full of friends, dancing, and enjoying the food scene in New York. They told the story of how as their feelings for each other deepened, while they realized how similar their values were, at the same time they saw increasingly that they had very different backgrounds. While to date they had always shared expenses, increasingly Tamera would suggest something—travel, a big wedding—that they could not afford if they shared the expense 50/50. At first Tamera said she would "loan" Manny the funds to pay half his share of a vacation. But upon their return, they both "felt silly" with creating a plan for paying it back. They realized something had to shift. They just could not imagine what would work for them. As they moved to formalize their partnership Tamera bumped up against the reality of her family wealth but did not know how to discuss it.

Family Membership

I suggested that Manny tell his family story first because Tamera had used more of the time during our first session. He came from a small nuclear/large extended family in Ecuador where his parents each ran a small business. They divorced, and money became contentious and secretive in the family. His mother asked for support, but his father refused. His father would ask Manny how his mother's business was doing. His mother expanded from one store to two without telling anyone. Manny and his two sisters felt the tug of war between his parents. While his sisters joined his mother's business, Manny was an exceptional student, and his community rallied around him. Many people in the town where he lived pooled funds to send him to school in Washington State. He continues to feel grateful and indebted to all of them. For a few months before he started school, he went to work for his uncle in the Southwest working at a farm. He saw the extremely hard lives faced by migrant workers and heard the histories of the conditions they fled and the hardships they faced. It solidified his values, and he arrived at graduate school "purpose driven," dedicated to creating sustainable and just agriculture.

Tamera also came from a family with divorced parents, though they handled money transparently and generously. Her father had family wealth, and her mother did not. While they were married, she felt that they treated their money as "theirs." She never heard them argue about money. When they divorced, her mother did not ask for much, and her father agreed to whatever she asked for. They remained genuinely friendly until her father died. The history of her family's handling money was much more strife ridden. Her great-grandfather on her father's side made a fortune in oil wells, which left her feeling very guilty. That branch of her family maintained the wealth but were involved in several public scandals. By the time the money came to her father and his two sisters they were a publicly known family. His sisters married men who both took their money and "invested" it in business ventures that failed. Both sisters' marriages ended in divorce. Tamera's father, the youngest, was embarrassed by his family and fearful of following in their footsteps so he lived an abstemious life. He spent little of his wealth on himself, garnered the respect of his community, and gave generously. When he died, he left a Trust for his only daughter that paid out annually. Because of his own fears and family history, however, he wrote a provision that did not allow Tamera control of the money until she was 50.

System Context

When a couple comes together, they navigate questions of how to come together and realign relationships with extended family to include one's spouse. Issues such as money, sex, and power require attention as well. The challenge of developing their interdependence becomes front and center. It often manifests through their approach to money. It is negotiated differently in every couple and influenced by culture, gender, and class. But whether they are compelled to write a pre-nuptial agreement, or are simply making their partnership legal, there are common hurdles and occurrences. They need to decide how much of their financial picture and decision-making to disclose to their partner and how much to keep private, or even secret. Some disclosures are unavoidable, as when people buying property are required to submit net worth statements. These disclosures and revelations bring up individuals' self-judgment, insecurities, fears, and values. While some couples consider the pre-nup a way to avoid dangers and pit falls within their relationship, others consider it an affirmative step toward achieving the relational dynamic they want.

Beginning Stage of Treatment

Their couple story involved an account of how they came together slowly and deliberately. They placed emphasis on individual identity and created a values statement about their union which included: Showing up in big and small ways. Not succumbing to conflict avoidance. Allowing for independence. Fostering ease, fun, and evolution.

We start to explore her feelings about the money she inherited. She says she feels like the money is "in a golden box" she only rarely uses. She says she feels guilty for the damage to the planet caused by how her family originally made the money and for using money she did not make. But she says, she also says she wants Manny to be able to enjoy it. Lastly, Tamera says she really wants to tell Manny how much money she has but is worried what will happen. Manny says he is not worried about seeing her any differently than he already does. He points out all the ways in which they have differences but says he believes those differences strengthen rather than weaken them. He has anxiety and finds that while it sometimes makes Tamera annoyed or anxious herself, most of the time he feels that she has compassion for him, and that that gives him compassion for himself. He says, "we own it together."

Twenty minutes before the end of the first session, Tamera says, "I have seven million dollars." I ask her how it feels to say it out loud. She says—"weird, but a relief, but weird." I ask where in her body she feels it, and she says, "there's a tightness in my chest." I ask Manny how he feels hearing it. He says "I don't think I've ever known someone with that much money. I don't know how I feel yet." I give them some homework, to look at the account statements from the bank where the money is managed. Tamera says, "oh I never even look at those" and Manny says, "I like numbers I'd be glad to."

When we next see each other, I ask what is going well. Manny says that he and Tamera asked for the bank statements and reviewed them. They are now more grounded in the actual numbers. As it turns out, Tamera will eventually be entitled to about $8 million dollars. I ask how they both feel. They both express feeling more grounded, and "real." They have not however gotten any further thinking about their pre-nup. I ask what is holding them up, but then stop and change course. I say, "never mind that, can you tell me what your idea of a pre-nup is." Tamera says, "well just what my money manager said, a document that protects me if we divorce." Manny says that he has never seen a pre-nup, so he really doesn't know. Manny says: I'd like to see examples. I ask if his lawyer has given him examples and he tells me he does not yet have a lawyer.

For these two people to truly come together in agreement, they need to level the playing field. I am explicit about that. They not only have differing amounts of money, they also have differing amounts of exposure to these concepts and documents. I recommend that he hire a lawyer—preferably a bi-lingual Spanish/English speaker, and that she/he gives Manny examples of pre-nups written in Spanish. He visibly relaxes and brightens up at the idea.

Change during Treatment

Tamera and Manny are very aware of their shared values and explicit about the relationship they want, and that helps them a great deal. Manny reports that having examples of a pre-nup, written in Spanish has been meaningful, and he now wants to figure out how to translate their shared values into the practical world. I suggest they look at the values template that we use in our workshops.

I give them new homework: imagine taking just the interest off the Trust, which is the amount Tamera is allowed to have. It is about $100,000 annually. I ask them to each make a list of what they would do with the funds. When they come back Manny reports he had lots of ideas, buying a new suit for their wedding, getting a new sofa, buy Tamera a pair of earrings, and paying back his family and community what he owes them for paying for graduate school. Tamera is stuck. All she could come up with was to pay for a bigger wedding. She says "I kept wishing I could ask my dad for permission to use the money. But it's mine! I wish I didn't feel like this." We play out what it would feel like for her to talk with her father, and what she thinks he would say to her. She tells him her worries about money. She tells him what she's doing now, for the environment fighting climate change. Lastly, she tells him about Manny (because they never met), and how much she thinks they would like each other. In her mind he tells her to go live a great life with Manny. It is an emotional experience, and a breakthrough.

Treatment Outcome

The couple starts to come together based on their shared values and shared vision for a life together. They wrest control of the pre-nup from their lawyers and ask for certain new unconventional provisions. They plan a big wedding with all the people they love, whom they feel have supported them in their lives. They also set out a budget for charitable giving to environmental causes they believe in, they pay back Manny's family and begin to pay back the members of his community, and they buy each other "fun fancy" gifts. Occasionally Manny and Tamera hear the voices in their head pulling back from engaging with their money. Manny will hear himself saying "that's what other people do, but not me" and Tamera will hear herself saying "maybe we shouldn't give that much away." When that happens, they both tell me, they have a new awareness that helps them correct themselves, and gives them a shared vocabulary they use with each other to stay aligned with their shared values and their vision for their life together.

Conclusion

The practicalities of money and class intertwine with their attached meanings to cause great complexities for families, couples, and individuals. Mental health practitioners know that the practical circumstances into which a person is born and raised have enormous influence on their internal lives, as do the narratives and meanings that build up around those circumstances. However, the practicalities of money and class and the narratives around them have been absent from mental health practice, in great part due to the social taboo of discussing money in our society. As we said earlier, we hope that the future will bring more thinking, research and writing on the sources of the taboo.

Throughout our careers we have been exploring ways to improve people's lives by guiding through this taboo. In designing the workshop, we found a way to quickly stimulate conversations about participants' relationship to money and class. We discovered that talking about money in multiple ways, with multiple people, and with intention and focus works to destigmatize money as a topic. This has brought awareness to the multiple threads of meaning of money for hundreds of people.

The workshop has allowed participants to strip away some of the emotional attachments enough so that the taboo of money talk is diminished. It has provided a blueprint for mental health professionals to use for themselves and their clients. It has expanded the universe of people who can be exposed to the healthier more functional experience of discussing money. It has been a catalyst for many people to change their relationship to money.

We realize that the positive result of the workshop experience is primarily a first-order change. We know the work has to continue. We are heartened from our follow up with participants who tell us that they are motivated to continue and expand upon the process. Some of them have signed up for further work with us to get deeper into the conversation. Others are asking for more professional guidance.

For the past two decades, Judith Stern Peck has been leading the research on money and family life at The Ackerman Institute for the Family. Throughout that time, with various collaborators, she has been working toward this objective. The following principles have evolved from the work. All of these ideas have been incorporated into the workshop design.

1. Create safety and positive language for facilitating money conversations
2. Pace and sequence the money conversations
3. Consider using values as a language tool
4. Begin to neutralize the emotional attachments as each surface
5. Explore personal money/class identity
6. Develop comfort with financial language
7. Look at family legacy around money/work/class
8. Address money conversation from multiple perspectives

These principles apply to both the personal and professional dimensions for the mental health provider or any other professional that is engaged in talking to families, couples or individuals about money. They can act as guidelines for pursuing the conversation and breaking the taboo.

Let's go back to Gene who we met in our introduction. To recap, he was distressed by his father's somewhat dictatorial manner relative to the financial support. Gene could not figure out how to have the conversation. Every time he broached the subject, his dad would just repeat his decision to stop the support. Their relationship was in a downward spiral and given Gene's professional stance, he definitely felt compelled to reverse that trajectory. In the money-focused genogram exercise, Gene recognized the relational pattern of dependency that had been perpetuated. He also realized his dad's desire to break that pattern and did not disagree. He differed with the plan not the objective! He was able to approach the subject with a newer understanding. He was better equipped to develop a more realistic plan with his dad. He actually decided to use email as a way to begin the conversation. He was able to show his dad what he had discovered and as a result, they were able to sit together to map out a reduction plan over time. Gene sent us a note to let us know what happened and reiterated how helpful it had been for him to Follow the Money! He was grateful that the workshop had been so beneficial for him.

For most of our participants, the idea of following the money became another access point for their clinical work. Throughout the workshop, they would comment on how the integration of money as a theme to explore was a new concept and additionally, such a valuable one!

They understood how following the money could neutralize the emotional attachments, surface the reality, expand the exploration of self, and lead to the relational dynamics. Ultimately, they understood how following the money would expand their clinical resources.

All this having been said, we hope that our work, our workshop, and our book are just the beginning of something new. We encourage you, our reader, to be generative. We hope that you integrate the book's foundational ideas and as a group can move this issue forward into a broader conversation. While we cannot predict how our workshop design will be used by our readers and practitioners, our great hope is that the ideas promoted in this book become a part of a shift in mental health practice that finally breaks the taboo of talking about class and money.

Bibliography

Ahrons, Constance R. "Divorce: An Unscheduled Family Transition." In *The Expanded Family Life Cycle: Individual, Family and Social Perspectives*, edited by Betty Carter and Monica McGoldrick, Boston: Allyn and Bacon, MA. 1999.

Bowen, Murray. *Family Therapy in Clinical Practice*. New York: Jason Aronson, 1978.

Bergerand, Brenda, and Stephanie Newman. *Money Talks: In Therapy, Society, and Life* (Psychoanalysis in a New Key Book Series). New York: Routledge, 2011.

Birnbaum, Philip. *Daily Prayer* Book. Ha-Siddur Ha-Shalem, Translated and Annotated with an Introduction. New York: Hebrew Publishing Company, 2002.

Brewster, Mary Kim, and Marcia Sheinberg. *ARA Manual Revision*, New York: Ackerman Institute, September 2015.

Cameron, Julia, *The Artist's Way Workbook*. New York: Jeremy P. Tarcher /Penguin, 1992, 2006.

Carter, Betty, and Monica McGoldrick, eds. *The Expanded Family Life Cycle: Individual, Family and Social Perspectives*. Boston: Pearson Allyn & Bacon, 2005.

Epstein, Mark. *Going on Being: Life at the Crossroads of Buddhism and Psychotherapy*. Somerville, MA: Wisdom Publications, 2008.

Epstein, Mark. *Psychotherapy Without the Self: A Buddhist Perspective*. New Haven, CT: Yale University Press, 2008.

Epstein, Mark. *Thoughts Without a Thinker: Psychotherapy from a Buddhist Perspective*. New York: Basic Books, 1995.

Goldstein, Joseph, and Jack Kornfield. *The Path of Insight Meditation*. New York: Shambhala, 1995.

Grubman, James. *Strangers in Paradise: How Families Adapt to Wealth Across Generations*. Turners Falls, MA: Family Wealth Consulting, 2013.

Hardy, Kenneth V. and Laszloffy, Tracy A., "The Cultural Genogram: Key to Training Culturally Competent Family Therapists." *Journal of Marital & Family Therapy* 21: 3 (1995): 227–37.

Housel, Morgan. *The Psychology of Money*. New York: Harriman House, 2022.

Kabat-Zinn, Jon. *Wherever You Go, There You Are*. New York: Hachette Books, 2023.

Kornfield, Jack. *The Wise Heart: A Guide to the Universal Teachings of Buddhist Psychology*. New York: Bantam Books, 2008.

McGoldrick, Monica, and Randy Gerson. *Genograms in Family Assessment*. New York: W.W. Norton, 1985.

Parker, Priya. *The Art of Gathering: How We Meet and Why It Matters*. New York: Riverhead Books, 2018.

Peck, Judith Stern. *Money and Meaning: New Ways to Have Conversations about Money with Clients*. Hoboken, NJ: John Wiley & Sons, Inc., 2008.

Peck, Judith Stern. "A Room of One's Own . . . and 500 Pounds." *Journal of Feminist Family Therapy* (Winter 1992).

Peck, Judith Stern, and Fredda Herz Brown, "Families in the Divorce and Post Divorce Process." In *Reweaving the Family Tapestry: A Multigenerational Approach to Families*, edited by Fredda Herz Brown. New York: W.W. Norton, 1991.

Peck, Judith Stern, and Jennifer Manocherian. "Divorce in the Changing Family Life Cycle." In *The Changing Family Life Cycle*, edited by Betty Carter and Monica McGoldrick. Boston, MA: Ally & Bacon.

Salzberg, Sharon. *Real Happiness*. New York: Workman Publishing Company, Inc., 2013.

Salzberg, Sharon, ed. *Voices of Insight*. Boulder, CO: Shambhala Publications, 1999.

Shapiro, Margaret. "Money: A Therapeutic Tool for Couples." *Family Process* 46 (September 2007): 279–92.

Sheinberg, M. "Navigating Treatment Impasses at the Disclosure of Incest: Combining ideas from Feminism and Social Constructionism." *Family Process* 31 (1992): 201–16.

Streib, Jessi. *The Power of the Past: Understanding Cross Class Marriages*. Oxford: Oxford University Press, 2020.

Watts-Jones, Thandiwe Dee. "Location of Self: Opening the Door to Dialogue on Intersectionality in the Therapy Process." *Family Process* 49 (2010): 405–20.

www.ingramcontent.com/pod-product-compliance
Ingram Content Group UK Ltd.
Pitfield, Milton Keynes, MK11 3LW, UK
UKHW021705230926
475560UK00015B/210

9 781538 183502